MW01531823

UNLOCKING
THE
CODE TO BLISS

Unlocking the Code to Bliss by Debbie Adams

Copyright © 2022 Debbie Adams

Interior Design by Gabriela Pears

Cover by Gabriela Pears.

UNLOCKING THE CODE TO BLISS
A Southern Belle's Secret

DEBBIE ADAMS

First and foremost I want to thank my Heavenly Father for directing me and giving me the wisdom to write this book.

I want to thank my husband Bud the love of my life for always letting me be me.

I want to thank Mom and Dad for always inspiring me to follow my dreams.

I want to thank my friend MarLycia my cheerleader for all of her support.

Last but not least I want to thank my special friends Mechelle Wollard, Michelle Nack, Teresa Burnett and so many other friends for your encouragement and support.

This book wouldn't have been possible without God's leading and wisdom and all of the encouragement and support. Thank You! Love You All!

Table of Contents

Introduction

This book is written in hopes that you will find Bliss in your life by learning new techniques on how to overcome struggles you may be having or that you may not even realize you're having.

If you're anything like me you might not even be aware of any struggles until you really think about the choices you have been making in your life. It really was an eye opener for me!

I didn't think I had bad eating habits and I hadn't ever needed to diet; however, the way I was choosing to eat was affecting my body and I wasn't even aware. We need to all be conscious of the decisions we're making and to be aware of what we're putting into our bodies.

God created us in His image and He created our bodies to work in a certain way where every part is connected together to create a balanced system.

My purpose for this book is to help you see and understand as I've learned over the past couple of years how God created us and how the things we put in our bodies affect everything and even our spirit and soul.

This book hopefully will show you how to find Bliss and become a better YOU! When you feel better physically, you're more at peace with yourself and will feel closer to God as you seek him.

CHAPTER 1

Definition Of Healthy And Why Be Healthy

As I was growing up I didn't think much about whether my body was healthy or not. I just knew I didn't get sick very often except for maybe a head cold or something minor. I knew people that stayed sick or were in the hospital quite often and I was just thankful I was well. My mom cooked all of the time and we lived on a farm and we had a garden so I probably thought that eating what my mom cooked was keeping me well. Like any typical child I played outside and got dirty from making mud pies and playing with frogs and all kinds of insects and drinking fresh water out of the hose pipe. In today's time since the so called pandemic started we all need to have hand sanitizer and Lysol to keep germs away. I don't remember using hand sanitizer growing up or being worried about getting sick like everyone seems to be nowadays. Maybe people just trusted God more and knew He created the immune system in their bodies and didn't worry as much back then. Were we healthier back in the good old days…I would think we probably ate better and took care of ourselves more but I'm sure there were still people that weren't well. There just wasn't as much talking about being healthy years ago like it is today. There's more media coverage now on how to lose weight and get healthy and more people are trying every new thing they find or hear about. Years ago people were busier with working their farms and when they did come in the house they didn't have much time for tv like we do now. People were more concerned about spending time with their families and praying and talking to God rather than listening to media 24/7 like we do now.

So what is the definition of being healthy? I looked up Webster's definition and according to Webster being healthy is "the condition of being free from illness and disease and the general condition of the body and a condition in which someone is thriving or doing well."Webster also defines healthy as "the condition of being sound in body, mind, or spirit." This definition is very true because if we're sound in our mind and spirit we will also be sound in our body. I'm sure we don't think about how all of this is connected together. Your spirit and body is affected by your soul. Our spirit and soul work together to help us find peace and joy and happiness in life. When our soul and spirit are at peace and our mind is where it needs to be then our body will be in the right place to be thriving. We need to keep our mind thinking right too because this world makes us see and think on things we don't need to be thinking on and a lot of times will get everything out of sync. We need to keep our mind on the correct things and the most important being God and His Word! Romans 12:2 "And be not conformed to this world: but be ye transformed by the renewing of your mind, that ye may prove what is that good, and acceptable, and perfect, will of God." We need to be transformed by the renewing of our mind and thus shaping ourselves from the inside to the outside. Our soul, spirit and mind is all connected to our body so to get fit we need to start from the inside at our soul and spirit and then move to our mind and body. Many times we might bring sickness into our bodies because our mind or spirit might not be sound. Think about that for a moment...

How many times do we allow stress to come into our lives and we all know that stress isn't good for our bodies. Sometimes I know stress can't be helped. There was one time I got so stressed over my Pastor having open heart surgery that my blood pressure sky rocketed and my doctor put me on medication and I had never been on blood pressure meds my entire life. I wasn't on them long though because when my mind and spirit got back in sync my body did also. So why did I allow my body to become so stressed that everything went out of sync. That was before I had even thought about how our bodies operate. I knew God designed them and God being a perfect God designed them in such a perfect way that each body part would operate in sync with every other body part. My body sure told me something was out of sync with the super high blood pressure. If I knew then what I know now maybe that wouldn't have even happened. Stress is never a good thing for our bodies even though it's always a part of our daily lives. Some people deal with it better than others and I deal with it better now than I did years ago. The National Cancer Institute defines stress as "the body's response to physical, mental, or emotional pressure. Stress causes chemical changes in the body that can raise blood pressure, heart rate, and blood sugar levels. It may also lead to feelings of frustration, anxiety, anger, or depression. Stress can be caused by normal life activities or by an event, such as trauma or illness. Long-term stress or high levels of stress may lead to mental and physical health problems."

If you're like me you probably haven't ever thought about how your mind and spirit is connected to your body. Learning is knowledge and power and since I've learned about how our bodies are created and connected I want you to learn about your body and I want YOU to get your body healthy and in turn be at peace and happy.

I'm sure whether you're a church goer or not you have heard about our Spirit in one way or another. We have a body, soul, and Spirit and they're all connected and what affects one affects the others. We need to keep them all in sync if we want to get healthy and stay fit. God created you in His image! Genesis 1:27 "So God created man in His own image, in the image of God created he Him; male and female created He them." You're in the image of God even though you have a human body so why not get your body healthy and keep it fit so you may honor God even more. God loves you and wants the best for you and so He wants you to be happy and healthy. Do you ever get down and maybe some days you don't feel good well maybe your body is trying to tell you something. Whether you realize it or not your body will give you signs that something isn't right and that's just the way it was designed. Like a well oiled machine your body and all of its systems should all operate smoothly together. You should be able to see and hear and walk with no problem but when something goes out of sync and you feel like something isn't right that's your body telling you to pay attention and get all systems in sync. God created you and your body in such a way that it's all connected together and what affects one affects all. We will talk more about this later.

So why are you wanting to get healthy...is it because someone told you you need to or you know you need to and want to. Unless you have a complete desire to get a healthy body you will only do it for a short time and stop. I want YOU to get healthy and stay fit and if you develop a healthy lifestyle like I've started doing over the past year you will have a healthy body, mind, and spirit. Like I said earlier I didn't even think about being healthy as a child but as I've become older and started eating the wrong things and making bad life choices I realized something needed to change. We can sometimes go through life thinking things are fine and maybe they are to a degree but needs tweaking in some areas and until we tweak these areas things won't change. Some people don't like change but we need to change in order to grow and be better than we were yesterday. Even as we're getting older we need to be more conscious and aware of how we are affecting our body, mind, and spirit. As we all know the older we get the more things seems to want to break down. We can help our bodies especially as we're getting older but also when we're young. I'm sure you've heard it said many times that you need to take care of yourself before you get older and that's true. Sometimes we don't take the best care of our bodies when we're younger but that doesn't mean you can't take care of them when you get older. Whatever your age why not commit yourself to having a healthy lifestyle. It's not all about what you can't eat as you see advertised on weight loss programs and I'm sure we've all tried them. Don't deny yourself the food you like just eat it in a different way.

They are plenty of things to add to how you eat to give you a healthy lifestyle. Take lemons for an example....did you know that even the rinds are good for you? We've all heard about putting lemons in water and how good that is for you and even the rinds are good for you. Web MD says "The vitamins, fiber, and plant compounds in lemons can provide essential health benefits. The pulp, rind, and juice are rich with vitamins that stimulate immunity and reduce the risk of disease. The soluble dietary fiber in lemon aids in healthy digestion." Web MD also says "lemons contain about 31 grams of Vitamin C, which is nearly double the amount of Vitamin C needed in your daily diet. Along with boosting immunity, this burst of Vitamin C can reduce your risk of stroke and heart disease with regular consumption." Lemons have more health benefits than I realized until last year when I started drinking lemon water and started trying to live a healthier lifestyle.

Being healthy and staying healthy can have a positive affect on all areas of your life. You will have more energy and want to do more and your attitude will be more positive and you will be able to control and handle stress better. Believe me before I started getting a healthy lifestyle I had no energy and I was tired all of the time and I just wasn't happy with myself.

Our bodies need a healthy balance of nutrients in order to get healthy and stay fit. In order to stay well we need to have a balanced body and we need to eat better and have a healthy lifestyle. You will see how healthy your body is by what you put into it. We might think sugar is good and all the donuts and cakes and everything with sugar might taste really good but it's not. Harvard Health says "sugar has a bittersweet reputation when it comes to health. Sugar occurs naturally in all foods that contain carbohydrates, such as fruits and vegetables, grains, and dairy. Consuming whole foods that contain natural sugar is okay. However, problems occur when you consume too much added sugar-that is, sugar that food manufacturers add to products to increase flavor or extend shelf life." In a study published in 2014 in JAMA Internal Medicine, Dr. Hu and his colleagues found an association between a high-sugar diet and a greater risk of dying from heart disease. Over the course of the 15-year study, people who got 17% to 21% of their calories from added sugar had a 38% higher risk of dying from cardiovascular disease compared with those who consumed 8% of their calories as added sugar. "Basically, the higher the intake of added sugar, the higher the risk for heart disease," says Dr. Hu.

Your body needs to maintain a sense of balance at all times if possible. My point is this.....pay attention to what your body intakes and that will help you to not only get fit but to maintain a healthy lifestyle.

If you're not staying healthy it can affect your whole body and you will be prone to more diseases and ailments. Not eating proper or exercising can often lead to heart issues and other ailments. Just because you're thin and not overweight doesn't mean you're healthy either. You can be thin and have bad eating habits and you won't be healthy. That was me because I've always been thin and never had a problem with my weight so was I healthy....No probably not. We might not have the perfect weight or size but hey we look better than the person across the street that's overweight. In reality being overweight or being thin has absolutely nothing to do with being healthy. Body weight is definitely not a good prediction of body health. Like we mentioned earlier being healthy isn't just your body it starts with your mind and spirit and goes to your body. When you hear someone talk about wanting to get healthy remember it's a 3 fold process which involves your mind, spirit, and body. We talked about sugar intake earlier and an over consumption of sugar can cause negative effects on your brain such as cognitive learning and memory loss. We often associate memory loss with older people but younger people can have memory loss too if they have too high of a sugar consumption. There's also the issue of inactivity and that's another indicator of not being healthy. Like I've said before getting fit starts with your inside and moves to the outside. You are what you eat! If you have bad eating habits then you won't be healthy until you change the way you eat. Eating a variety of healthy foods will help to protect you from chronic illnesses.

I mentioned that I had bad eating habits before and that's probably where I got my cancer 14 years ago. I was drinking at least 4 cokes a day and we all know they're loaded with sugar. I learned from talking with my doctor that cancer feeds on sugar and oh my goodness my body had a high consumption rate of sugar. There were several things I changed in my eating when I got cancer but I still wasn't healthy. I was drinking large amounts of caffeine and not necessarily in coffee because caffeine is In a lot of different things we eat and drink. Caffeine isn't good for your body either because it can cause blood pressure problems and other issues if you have large consumptions of it. You're probably thinking well everything I eat or drink can cause problems so why should I want to get healthy? It has to all be in the amount of consumption. A big caffeine problem is with those Energy Drinks and I've never had any but had friends that drank them! They're supposed to give you extra energy and keep you awake but they're loaded with extra amounts of caffeine per the small fluid ounces. Some are even at a dangerous level. If you are drinking those I would be extremely careful. I hope you're getting the idea that getting healthy isn't just what you eat or drink but that it's a whole mindset that starts from the inside and that you can still have your favorite foods but just in lower consumptions added to more healthy meals.

Also to get healthy you need to eat a balanced meal and try to have a set time when you eat your meals.

Being healthy means different things to different people. To some it might be losing weight and to others it might be getting more energy to do things. Whatever is your idea of being fit we all need to strive to get our bodies in sync and stay healthy. In essence means that you're experiencing vitality and feel strong and confident. You don't have to give up the food you love as long as you're eating healthy at least 80% of the time. I try to eat healthy mostly during the week and Saturday is my "free" day to eat what I want and what I love. We love Pizza and Mexican so we usually eat it on Saturdays. Healthy habits are what reinforces your positive attitude and awareness. Deciding to eat healthy is the first step toward creating a long term healthy routine. It will be hard at first at least it was for me but when you get it as part of your daily routine toward getting healthy it will get easier. There's so many short term fads out there to try and from anyone I've talked to these fads never last very long. To make it a lifestyle change for getting healthy and staying fit you need to start off slowly to make it a new habit rather than the many fads of today. Being healthy just means you're making the correct choices and it involves more than healthy eating. Go outside and enjoy the sunshine and get some Vitamin D from the sun and get a good night's sleep and stop worrying over things you can't control. Being healthy just means that you feel motivated to find ways to get fit. Being healthy is essentially a mindset that you need to keep re-evaluating and might need to fine tune.

Healthy means you pay attention to your relationship with your body. Healthy is recognizing and seeing everything your body can do not what size you are. Healthy is eating foods because they nourish you. Healthy is getting a good night's sleep and doing self care. Healthy is a fundamental awareness of what's good for you. It's saying no to things because you know your boundaries. It's about loving and appreciating your body. It's about being kind to yourself because we mess up and we need to grow from it. Healthy is looking at the big picture because it's so much more than just eating and exercising. You can be healthy physically but mentally still feel bad. Having a healthy mind is not being oppressed by it and with a healthy mind you can just throw off the negative thoughts. Being healthy is a constant process not a goal you accomplish and then check it off. A healthy person is positive, optimistic. helpful, energetic, and open minded. Health is one of the most important factors of life and being healthy makes you more happy and peaceful with life. What's important when you are trying to become healthy is how you feel mentally and physically. Being healthy isn't a mold for everyone to fit into it's about finding your definition of healthy where you can thrive physically, mentally, and spiritually.

CHAPTER 2

How Is Your Body Designed

We talked about how your body is connected to your mind and spirit. Did you know that your body no matter what shape or size is a temple of the Holy Spirit and we can glorify God with our body by keeping it healthy.

1 Corinthians 6:19-20 "Know ye not that your body is the temple of the Holy Spirit which is in you, which ye have of God, and ye are not your own? For ye are bought with a price: therefore glorify God in your body, and in your spirit, which are God's."

God is the one that created our bodies and so He knows how He designed them to work and operate. God designed our bodies to be in balance and we (myself included) have loaded our bodies down with so much stuff they're not healthy anymore. That's why occasionally we have to do a renewal on not only our minds but our whole body.

Romans 12:1-2 "I beseech you therefore, brethren, by the mercies of God, that ye present your bodies a living sacrifice, holy, acceptable unto God, which is your reasonable service.

And be not conformed to this world: but be ye transformed by the renewing of your mind, that ye may prove what is that good, and acceptable, and perfect, will of God." Sometimes we have to do a renewal in order to get away from bad habits and to become a better YOU! I've had to do this recently and I was getting in a rut and I knew something needed to change. Sometimes when you change the way you do things you have a whole new outlook on life at least I did. Even changing the way you eat can make a big difference in your outlook. You don't have to deny yourself food if you find new ways to eat the food you love. You might not need to lose weight you might just need to renew your body and to get more energy. That's what happened to me....by renewing my spirit and changing things around in how I did things it gave me more energy and it was definitely a game changer when I changed to a healthier lifestyle.

Have you ever wondered how your body actually works? Like we mentioned before your body was created by God and He created it in such a way that every single part works with all of the body parts. God created something so small like your cells and you can't see them but they communicate with your body. Did you know your cells produce the energy your body needs? Some cells carry oxygen throughout your body while other fight infection. Cleveland Clinic says "Red blood cells bring oxygen to the tissues in your body and release carbon dioxide to your lungs for you to exhale. Oxygen turns into energy, which is an essential function to keep your body healthy." When cells work together for a specific function it's called tissue. When 2 or more tissue work together it's called an organ. There are many systems that interact with each other every second of the day to keep your body moving. Just think how amazing our body is that God created! Your body was created to be in balance and it's just we as humans don't pay attention to our bodies when they try to tell us that we're not doing things to keep it well. All of us have developed bad habits (myself included) that led to bad choices that resulted in unhealthy lifestyles. We all need to think more on how our body was created to operate to fight off diseases and to process the food we eat in order to stay balanced. In some cases our body might have gotten into overdrive from making bad life choices and we're making our body work harder than it needs to trying to maintain all it does on a daily basis. Your body was designed to be in balance and so it does a lot of detoxing in order to try to maintain healthiness. You can make small changes one at a time to improve your overall health. Try drinking water and get outside to enjoy the fresh air and try getting adequate sleep and you will be surprised the difference it will make in how you feel. Your skin is the last place to receive nutrients and when your body is healthy inside it will show on the outside through your skin. The health of your skin and hair and nails looks better when you're eating right. When we eat for health our outward appearance will reflect our inner health. Like we said before start with the inner and work outward.

God designed your body in such a way that it all works together in some fashion or form. We all took science in school and learned about all of our bones and joints and tendons and muscles and how this bone is connected to that bone and so on. So what does all of this science stuff have to do with getting your body where it needs to be you ask. Because until you can understand how your body is connected and how it works you won't fully understand how being well or not being healthy will affect your body. Each part of your body is all dependent on the rest of your body to function. Your brain tells your heart to beat and God gives you another day to live with each heartbeat. Your nutrients from your digestive system gives you strong and healthy bones. Are you starting to get the picture? It's not us and what we do that keeps our bodies working, it's God and how He designed our bodies so perfectly to work that each muscle, tissue, cell, bones and many other body parts keep each other moving and operating to peek function. When we get sick our bodies have an immune system designed by God to protect us and to heal us naturally. John Hopkins defines our immune system as "The immune system protects your body from outside invaders. These include germs such as bacteria, viruses, and fungi, and toxins (chemicals made by microbes). The immune system is made up of different organs, cells, and proteins that work together." During the so called pandemic I was trusting my immune system to keep me well and it did it's job and my body stayed well.

I Corinthians 12:12 "For as the body is one, and hath many members, and all the members of that one body, being many, are one body: so also is Christ."

Your body was wonderfully created by God and everything is connected so perfectly and that's how it all works together so perfectly.

As we talked about earlier even the cells in your body help with your oxygen. You need oxygen to breathe and have energy and being well will give you more energy and stamina. Think about how God created all of your bones, tendons, and muscles to work. They all had to be placed a certain way in order for your legs and arms to bend and for you to be able to walk. According to John Hopkins "Bone provides shape and support for the body, as well as protection for some organs. Bone also serves as a storage site for minerals and provides the medium—marrow—for the development and storage of blood cells." You might wonder what does being healthy have to do with your bones. Well it has a lot to do with your bones. No bones about it (no pun intended) what you eat affects your bone vitality. I'm sure we all remember being told as children growing up to drink your milk so you will have strong bones and there's a lot of truth in that statement. Milk gives your bones much needed calcium and as we get older we know how important it is to keep our bones strong. Chester County Hospital says "Not only do many veggies have calcium, but they also have important nutrients such as magnesium, potassium and vitamin K that are also important for healthy bones." It's important to consider your bone health when your trying to find ways to get your body more balanced. Not enough physical activity can affect your bones as well. So get outside and walk around the block and get some Vitamin D as well as helping your bones by exercising.

So you're wanting to get healthy so what about your heart....it needs to be strong and balanced as well. We've all either had someone or had it ourselves where our heart was having problems. Keeping your heart healthy involves a lot of what we've been talking about such as stress, exercise, and eating right, and getting a good nights sleep. Stress isn't good for anybody and it's definitely not good for your heart. Stress will most times cause a faster heart rate and it's not good when your heart is having to overwork. So try to keep your stress at a minimal for your heart. Also don't overeat because that's not good for your heart either. On a positive note though chocolate and wine are actually good for your heart but only in moderation. I don't drink wine but I do eat plenty of chocolate. The most important thing about keeping your heart healthy is to keep exercising because your heart is a muscle and any exercise will strengthen it. My husband had a heart bypass and that's one thing they wanted him to do was walk and exercise to strengthen his heart. Keeping your heart strong is something you can work on everyday. The Heart Foundation says "A diet full of a variety of fruit and vegetables is linked to healthier hearts and a lower risk of heart disease." So I hope you're seeing a pattern here in that getting healthy isn't just to lose weight or get more energy it's an overall process and it involves your whole body and spirit. You have to consider not only your bones but also your heart and basically every part of your body because it's all connected.

The one thing we haven't talked about yet is your brain and all of its interconnecting parts or your operating system as I like to call it. Just like a computer with all of its hardware our brain operates all of our body's inter workings. Our brain is actually composed of billions of nerve cells that are arranged in a unique pattern. Your brain is like a highway of nerve cells all connected to your body. Your brain's operating system tells your body what to do similar to a computer's operating system. Think about how many times your eyes blink well your brain tells your eyes when to blink. Your brain controls every aspect of your body and your ability to function in your daily life. We need to be concerned about our brain vitality just like we're concerned about our heart health. With a strong and vital brain we're constantly getting new nerve cell connections and old ones are being repaired. Our brain is constantly changing as as we're having new experiences and new learning put in our operating systems. Brain health is important at any age but is really important as we begin to get older. Brain vitality can help you to maintain your memory as well as your understanding and communication. We need to be keeping our brain well with challenging mental activities such as reading, doing crosswords, crafts and anything to keep your brain engaged. There is a lot of mental decline such as dementia and Alzheimer's so keeping your brain well is important too.

Taking care of your body and getting healthy and maintaining a balanced life style is more than just losing some weight or getting more energy it involves your whole body and every part of it from your head to your toe. It even includes the breath you take and thank the Lord you're able to take another breath each day. When you're well you don't get out of breath as quickly as when you're not. I know before I changed to living a healthier lifestyle and eating correctly I was out of breath after not doing much at all. When you're eating right and exercising and getting rid of bad habits you enjoy life more. I enjoy walking outside and I'm able to fully enjoy doing more things. Dr. Shalu Ramchandani, a health coach and internist at the Harvard-affiliated Benson-Henry Institute says "breathing isn't only life-sustaining; it can be life-enhancing when used as a tool." We talked about stress earlier and deep breathing can help reduce stress. I've had people tell me before to take a deep breath when I was aggravated about something and now I can see why. Simple breathing exercises throughout the day can actually help you. I do know whenever I take deep breaths it does make me feel better about whatever was aggravating me. So why not try it just don't think about anything and slowly breathe in and exhale out and see if it doesn't calm your body and spirit.

It's just miraculous to me thinking about how God created our bodies and covering all of our body parts with our skin and covering our heads with our hair and how are nails grow without much effort. Psalms 139:14 - "I will praise thee; for I am fearfully and wonderfully made: marvellous are thy works; and that my soul knoweth right well." When you have healthy skin and hair and nails you can just see it. Have you noticed people how their face glows and their hair is oh so shiny well that's a sign of good vitality and wellness. Drinking lots of water is a good way to keep your hair, skin, and nails healthy. Our bodies need water for all of our organs, tissues, and cells to work effectively. It's been recommended to drink 8 glasses a day to flush out toxins and to stay hydrated. I drink water every day maybe not 8 glasses but I do drink a lot of water. If you're not drinking water why not try it and see what it can do for your hair, skin, and nails. Another thing is to get a good nights sleep and the recommended hours is 7-9 and that's when you're body is renewing itself so the longer you can sleep the better. Stop biting your nails! How many times was I told growing up to stop biting my nails and I didn't realize until I had gotten older that biting your nails weakens them and causes damage to not only your nails but to the skin around them. Using conditioner on your hair will also make your hair look shiny. Doing a oil treatment on your hair will help too. The main thing about your hair, nails, and skin is to Drink Water and plenty of if and to get a Good Night's Sleep! Water will flush out any toxins in your body and refresh you and sleeping good will get you renewed while you sleep.

Now let's talk about your organs and how to keep them well. You might not think too much about your organs but we need to consider them too when trying to get healthy. We all know from science class in school that organs have a specific function and structure and there are organs all over our body. First and foremost a balanced diet and exercise is essential to have vitality in your organs. To have a balanced diet you would need to eat a moderate proportion of carbohydrates, proteins, vitamins, fats, minerals, and water. There are five organs that are critical and needs to be kept well for survival and these are the brain, heart, liver, kidneys and lungs. Keeping these organs healthy and happy are essential. Every organ depends on the others to work properly and that's why we need to keep up the wellness in all of our organs. Our organs are hidden from view in our bodies but they're very indispensable. Each organ in your body is a little different from each other and you can tailor your lifestyle to give all of your organs the attention it needs and in that way keeping all of your organs well. Your heart is the one organ that pumps blood to all parts of your body so if this organ isn't balanced and well it could be fatal. Your kidneys are responsible for maintaining the whole body. Sometimes one of your kidneys may go bad and you might need a kidney transplant. Your brain only takes up a small percentage of your body but it's running the show sorta speak because without your brain what will you be able to do. That's why for these major organs at least it's very essential to keep them balanced and happy.

We've been talking about how God created your body and talked about all of your basic body parts and how to get wellness and how it needs to start from the inside and go out. The one thing we haven't talked about is your mind. You can say you're going to start a healthy lifestyle and never do it because you haven't set your mind to do it. You can talk yourself out of doing almost anything. So how do your get your mind balanced so you can start getting your body healthier. First and foremost you need to get all the negative thoughts out of your mind like those that tell you it's too hard and you can't do it because you can do it. I have to admit I didn't jump on the bandwagon at first to get healthier and my mind was convincing me not to but I decided to totally commit to it and I'm glad I did. Unless you commit to doing it you won't be able to keep it up. Your brain is what will decide for you whether you decide to have a balanced lifestyle or not. It's all about mind control and making the right choices for your life. You know that you need to get healthier and only you have the power to decide whether to do it or not. A simple way to boost your brain power and mind control is to exercise and then you will be on your way to better wellness. Mind control is in essence recognizing that you have the power and control to make the best decisions for your body. You train your thoughts just like you would train anything else. It's all about mind control! By learning new thinking patterns, you can literally improve every aspect of your body, health, weight, strength, and fitness goals.

CHAPTER 3

Gut Health And
Why Worry About Your Gut

Your gut and how it digests what you eat has a lot to do with your overall wellness and well being. If we take in foods that are bad for us then your gut will have a harder time digesting and will make it hard on your overall body. Remember in getting a balanced body it starts with the inside and works outward. We not only have to start with our Spirit and work outward toward our body but we need to start inward on our gut and work outward. Remember how our skin will be glowing when our body is in balance. Well if we eat right where our gut can digest correctly it will go out to our skin making it glow. Have you ever noticed that when you feel good inside then you feel good all over? Well that's the same concept....get your gut healthy and it will proceed to your whole body. It might seem like a slow process but you take it one step at a time and one part of your body at a time. Your gut and stomach are similar in that they both do digestion and your gut does a little more than digest it also breaks down and absorbs nutrients from our food. Have you ever had your stomach hurt after eating something....well it could be that your gut wasn't able to break it down enough and then when your stomach tried to do it's part of digesting it wasn't able to do it properly.

So I hope you're seeing why keeping your gut clean and well is so important.

Your gut is basically the foundation of everything. It aids in the digestion of the foods you eat, absorbs nutrients, and uses it to fuel and maintain your body.

Your gut is your gastrointestinal (GI) system, and the health of your gut is determined by the levels and types of bacteria in your digestive, intestinal tract. There is good bacteria and bad bacteria and your gut needs to have good bacteria in order to function properly and to be fit and in sync with the rest of your body.

Did you know that your gut health affects everything in your body? The gastrointestinal system takes in and processes nutrients, and is also a communication center and disease fighter. From your immune systems to your digestive function, a healthy gut plays a big role in your overall well-being.

The gut covers the parts of the body involved with food input and output. Gut health is the bacteria in the microbiome, and this is all in your large intestine. Your good bacteria feeds on fiber, including both soluble and insoluble fiber in our diets. The bad bacteria feed on elements in simple sugars and processed foods. Our body has an important relationship with our microbiome: it takes in all these microorganisms, digests them and then produces other compounds that our body can use. So, while some of these bacteria are harmful and others are beneficial, they both need to be there.

Gut balance also has an effect on your brain. Serotonin the hormone that makes us feel happy is produced in the gut. That's why psychological stress can negatively affect your gut health, causing inflammation and emotional eating. Because the gut has such a strong connection with so many other parts of our body and our well-being, it's important to keep it healthy.

According to the National Institute of Health, "digestive diseases affect 60 to 70 million Americans, ranging from gallstones and irritable bowel syndrome (IBS) to Crohn's disease and ulcerative colitis." So I hope you can see that gut related issues can go beyond your GI tract.

We've been talking about your gut health so what does gut health really mean? How does it affect the other parts of your body? What can you do to help your gut health if it's out of balance?

UC Davis Health describes gut health as

"the function and balance of bacteria of the many parts of the gastrointestinal tract. Ideally, organs such as the esophagus, stomach and intestines all work together to allow us to eat and digest food without discomfort."

Your body is connected together more than you may realize. God created your body in such a way that it will be connected and work together. "Digestion is one of the most important physiological functions of the body," says gastroenterologist Ashkan Farhadi,

MD. He also says, "As a prerequisite of absorption, digestion prepares the food to be transported across the body boundaries in our gut. Without digestion, our body cannot access nutrients that we consume and we will be starved."

Because your gut has such a strong connection with so many other parts of our well-being, it's important to keep it healthy.

To get your gut health in balance where it needs
to be try these tips.

Eat more fruits and vegetables.
Eat nuts
Eat whole grains
Eat prebiotic and probiotic foods

I never cared that much for fruits until I started thinking about what I was putting in my body. Fruits are good for you and are a good source of vitamins. Bananas even help with your potassium. I even started eating dried fruit in a bag and that way I always have fruit with me to eat for a snack.

Nuts are something I never liked even though they're a good source of protein. I did however find chocolate covered almonds and I love them and so now I can eat nuts in a different way and still get my protein. You can always find different ways to fit your lifestyle and still get the nutrients your body needs.

You can get your whole grains from bread, brown rice, oats, and even cereal. I eat oatmeal every morning and usually with some kind of fresh fruit in it.

The prebiotics your body needs is broccoli and apples and bananas. The probiotics you need is and sauerkraut. I do try and eat yogurt almost every day. You can also get over the counter probiotics if you think you're not eating enough.

I hope you're starting to see and understand why your gut health is so important and why we need to keep it well.

Digestion affects more than just your gastrointestinal health. Your gut is a communication center for the brain and it can affect other important health functions such as mental health. Dr. Farhadi says. "The lack of proper digestion can not only result in irritability, lack of energy and weakness, it may also affect our mood and overall sense of happiness." Digestive issues can affect how good you feel about yourself. Having a proper balance of gut bacteria affects your digestion, and when that balance is off, it can also weaken your immune system.

Immune cells in the gut interacts with the array of bacteria that lives in the GI tract and are influenced by our diet and lifestyle. The foods we eat affect the bacteria in our gut and in turn will affect the cells in our immune system. So it's very important to make sure we eat the right things that our gut needs. Like we talked about before our gut has good bacteria and bad bacteria and it needs more good bacteria to properly digest what we eat.

The gut and the immune system support one another to promote a healthy body. When they are in good relations, the body is equipped to respond to pathogens and to tolerate harmless bacteria, preventing an autoimmune response and ensuring overall well-being. The intestinal lining of your gut is delicate, and when it is weakened, you are more vulnerable to new harmful invaders. When your gut is out of balance and it doesn't have enough good friendly bacteria your whole body is affected. Improving your diet by cutting out processed foods and having more probiotics can help restore the composition of your gut and allows for a more efficient gut and immune system.

We've been talking about how your gut works and how to keep it in balance so that it will work properly. So another word you often hear is having a clean gut which is basically the same as your gut being in balance because if your gut is clean it will be able to work properly. It will be able to digest and get rid of bad toxins in your body if it's clean or in balance. Think of it this way.....when we're not loaded down with things we're able to function better in our daily lives and our bodies are the same way. So let's keep our guts clean and balanced so that our whole body will be able to function better on a daily basis.

A clean gut contributes to a strong immune system, a healthy heart and brain and so you're in a better mood and spirit and you have balanced digestion and you're able to get a restful night's sleep. A clean gut will also help in fighting away diseases.

In this day and age we're consuming a lot of junk food which is the highly processed and unnatural food in all the fast food restaurants we love. Do we really know what's in that food and yet we're putting it in our bodies. I'm like you and I love fast food but it's not good for your body if you're not also eating good foods to offset it. Too much junk food (toxins) will destroy the good bacteria in our gut. Balance is the key to keeping more good than bad bacteria in our gut. By watching what we eat and eating foods that put nutrients in our body we will continue to have a clean gut.

Now let's talk about the good foods to eat that are good for your gut. So who doesn't likes Chocolate? Yes I'm a chocolate lover and did you know that chocolate is good for your gut....well it is.

Chocolate can produce the good bacteria in our guts that we need and can also reduce inflammation. The best chocolate for your gut is dark chocolate. I know the milk chocolate might taste better but let's start eating some dark chocolate to get our guts balanced.

Louisiana State University researchers reported, that certain bacteria in the stomach feed on dark chocolate and ferment it into anti-inflammatory compounds that are good for the heart. Maria Moore, an undergraduate student and one of the study's researchers, explained it in a press release: "We found that there are two kinds of microbes in the gut: the 'good' ones and the 'bad' ones. The good microbes, such as Bifidobacterium and lactic acid bacteria, feast on chocolate," she said. "When you eat dark chocolate, they grow and ferment it, producing compounds that are anti-inflammatory." As an added health benefit why not add some fruit that's also good for you to your dark chocolate. Dark chocolate is loaded with nutrients to positively affect your health. Made from the seed of the cacao tree, it's one of the best sources of antioxidants. We know that we need antioxidants in our bodies because they prevent or delay damage to our cells and that's always a good thing. So anything we can eat that is an added health benefit for our bodies we should be eating.

Now we're going to talk about olive oil. Until recently I never thought much about the different oils we use to cook with or add to our foods. Did you know that olive oil is good for your gut? Olive oil is a fatty acid that absorbs really well in your gut and it also contains antioxidants. I've started cooking with olive oil and even putting some in the vegetables we eat. Olive oil is the healthiest and most nutritious cooking fat.

Liz Weinandy, lead dietitian at the Ohio State University Wexner Medical Center, says "there is research to show the microorganisms in our gut can break down the beneficial compounds in olive oil and improve our gut health," This is important because we know there are a lot of functions the gut microbiome plays on our overall health."

Olive oil is the natural oil extracted from olives and anything in its natural form is good for you. It also contains vitamins and that's something your body needs. Health line says "scientists estimate that the oleocanthal in 3.4 tablespoons (50 ml) of extra virgin olive oil has a similar effect as 10% of the adult dosage of ibuprofen." Olive oil it seems is a fighter of anti-inflammatory and that's a good thing. Olive oil can also help fight diseases and to keep your heart healthy. It seems olive oil has a lot of healthy benefits.

We mentioned about eating nuts and how nuts are good for you. I bet you didn't know that eating nuts is good for your gut too. Anything that you can eat that's good for your gut will also help the rest of your body. Remember how we've been saying the gut is connected to your brain and so whatever affects your gut will also affect other parts of your body. Like we've been saying in order to get fit it starts from the inside and works toward the outside. I hope you're seeing how the foods we eat and are putting in our bodies affect our overall health.

Nuts and their high fiber content as well as the antioxidant and anti-inflammatory properties are beneficial for your gut. Nuts fiber content is a prebiotic which feeds on the probiotic that's in your gut. I'm not much on eating nuts like my husband is but I do love dark chocolate covered almonds. Chocolate and nuts just seem to go together! We've already seen how our gut has a direct impact on our overall body and we've seen how some things we need to avoid eating. Nuts of any kind and even the skins are good for our health and they're a healthy snack.

When you include nuts (almonds, walnuts, cashews, and any kind) in your diet you're providing your gut with the good bacteria it needs and in turn your digestive system gets a boost. So with the good bacteria (microbiota) you're giving your gut you now have the vitamins and nutrients you need to have your gut well balanced and functioning properly.

Yogurt is good for our guts too. The best yogurt is the Greek ones and the organic ones. You wouldn't think that yogurt would be good for you because it's a fermented food; however, yogurt contains a lot of probiotics that's good for your digestive system.

We talked about digestion earlier and so anything to give it a boost always helps. Yogurt (the right kind) is rich in nutrients that your body needs and by eating it everyday (and I usually do) will help to boost your health. While it benefits your digestive system it can also help in weight management.

"Yogurt is a healthy addition to the diet because it contains calcium, protein, and active cultures," said Lori Rosenthal, MS, RD, CDN, a registered dietitian at the Montefiore Medical Center in New York.

When you're buying yogurt make sure and look at the ingredients to make sure it has active and live cultures in it because this is what will help you. Stay away from the yogurts that have processed sugars because that won't help you at all. You can get plain yogurt and add fresh fruit and you will get a great taste and a double benefit since fruit is also good for you. Whatever yogurt you decide on make sure it has live active cultures and no processed sugars. The Greek yogurt I get doesn't have any sugar content. In order to be beneficial for your body it needs to have the proper amount of calcium and proteins and active live cultures. Yogurt with vitamin D and 200 mg of calcium is the best choice for your gut.

CHAPTER 4

Intermittent Fasting and Exercise

Now we're going to talk about intermittent fasting and I'm wondering how many of you have done this. I've heard about people who prayed and fasted and I've always thought I couldn't do that because I would be starving not being able to eat. When I heard about intermittent fasting though it was different and I knew I could do this. It's an alternative day fasting and periodic fasting and you're timing your meals. You only eat every 8 or 10 hours and you decide what works best for you. . This kind of fasting anyone can do and it's good for your body too.

According to metabolic expert Dr. Deborah Wexler, associate professor at Harvard Medical School, "there is evidence to suggest that the circadian rhythm fasting approach, where meals are restricted to an eight to 10-hour period of the daytime, is effective." But still she recommends that people "use an eating approach that works for them and is sustainable to them."

If you're pregnant or nursing you might not need to be skipping meals. You need to choose what is best for you.

Intermittent fasting has been known to stabilize blood sugar levels and even decrease stress. It's also good for brain health and memory. It has good benefits but you decide if it's for you.

If you have medical conditions like diabetics or heart disease you might need to check with your doctor before you start intermittent fasting just to be on the safe side. For those of you that don't already have medical issues you can decide what is best for you. It's called intermittent because you will only eat every 8 or 10 hours.

If you're just starting I would start slow and gradually go up to the 10 hours. The time you're sleeping is also considered in your fasting time. You can eat dinner at 6pm and not eat anything else and then sleep all night and eat breakfast at 6am and that will be a 12 hour fast. You decide what schedule works best for you and your body.

There are also side effects just like anything because your body will need to get used to your new routine. These side effects usually go away.

The side effects are:

Hunger

Fatigue

Insomnia

Nausea

Headaches

Some people won't have any side effects but I wanted to list them. The most I ever had was slight hunger and headaches.

Overall I've had good benefits with intermittent fasting. It's probably as good if not better than regular diets in reducing calories.

There are benefits of intermittent fasting and it's more than just a fad diet. I'm sure if you're like me you want something long term and something that will last. So we've been talking about what we eat but did you know that when we eat is just as important? Breakfast has long been known as the most important meal of the day. It doesn't matter what time you have breakfast since it's the meal that breaks your fast of sleeping. It replenishes your body and starts your digestive process and refuels your body for the rest of the day.

We need to eat to live and not live to eat. That's the way I was because I was eating all the time. I had to change my routine and the way I was eating. I was definitely making bad choices in the way I was eating and when I changed my eating routine it was an eye opener. I saw that I had more energy and it seemed my whole body was happier. Now I'm eating to live and just because food is there doesn't mean I have to eat it. There are certain times during the day I eat and my body likes my new routine and my healthy lifestyle.

Now let's talk about some of the benefits and how it can help you and your body be more fit. Do you realize that when you're doing intermittent fasting that you're detoxing your body. If you're eating all of the time your body is continually having to digest so sometimes your body needs to

take a break. We've talked about how your gut and brain are connected, well you can help your brain by doing intermittent fasting. When you give your brain a detox you're boosting it and can help it in several ways. So fasting not only helps your body but also your mind. It clears your mind and improves brain functioning.

Rahul Jandial, MD, PhD "I recommend it for anyone who wants to improve their mood and hit peak cognition."

Whether you realize it or not, you already fast. After you've had dinner and before you eat breakfast you're sleeping and thus fasting. You might not think of sleeping as fasting but it is. So by fasting you can not only promote brain health but also lose weight. It can clear brain fog and sharpen your mind and believe me it sure helps me to think better when I'm fasting.

Another benefit is a better night's sleep. I'm sure we've all ate a heavy meal and then when we went to sleep it was as if we were in a sleep coma. Well your body is having to digest all you ate while you're sleeping. I've heard most of my life that you don't need to eat late and most say don't eat past 6pm. Well I never thought much about it until I started studying how our bodies work, and realized that all of my late night eating was actually harming my body. That's when I knew it was time for a change.

If we try and go to sleep on a full stomach it does two things. First, it will interfere with proper digestion. Second it might give you heartburn and so you will have a hard time sleeping. So if we eat earlier in the night, our bodies will be able to digest our food before we go to sleep and we will sleep better and wake up feeling refreshed.

We all get those late night cravings and as long as you get snacks that are easy to digest like grapes or yogurt, then you will still be able to get a good nights sleep. Always remember to stay hydrated and drink plenty of water while you're fasting too. As long as you're having routine eating patterns during the day you should be able to rest better at night.

Another benefit is weight loss. Some people like myself might not need to lose a lot of weight. You can also trim up to make yourself look better and feel better. No matter if you want to only lose a few pounds or if you want to lose a lot of weight intermittent fasting can help you. You can lose around 7-11 pounds in about 2 months.

"One of our main findings was that people who do

intermittent fasting lose about the same amount of weight as people on a regular calorie-restriction diet that cuts out 500 calories a day," says Krista Varady, PhD, researcher and professor of nutrition at the University of Illinois, Chicago. It can help with your metabolic health as well. It can lower your blood pressure as well as cholesterol and we all need to keep a check on these. Metabolic means your body is responding to food in a beneficial way and reduces your risk of medical conditions such as heart disease. It enhances hormone function to help you lose weight. Intermittent fasting helps you eat fewer calories while boosting your metabolism. It's a very effective tool to lose weight. It boosts your metabolic rate (increases calories output) and reduces the amount of food you eat (reduces calories intake).

Intermittent fasting is considered a very popular weight-loss method, and it has a lot of benefits. It can help you live a longer and all-around healthier life too. Anything that gives you a healthier lifestyle should also give you a longer life span. It's more about limiting when you eat rather than what you eat.

The main benefits from intermittent fasting are:

weight loss and fat burning

longer life span

protection against certain diseases

improved insulin resistance

cellular repair

hormonal balance

Remember when you're fasting to always stay hydrated. You can drink water, tea, and black unsweetened coffee. Avoid artificial sweeteners as they can affect your blood sugar. Drink things with very few calories. During the periods when you do eat, try to eat a healthy diet rich in whole grains, fruits, vegetables, and lean protein. Many people try intermittent fasting because they want to improve their health. While you're fasting, your body switches from burning sugar to burning fat for energy. This is very beneficial for your body.

Your body breaks down the food you eat into sugar, or glucose, for energy. When food is absent for an extended period of time, your body instead breaks down fat to release another energy source called ketones. This is what is referred to as a metabolic switch, and research suggests that alternating between using glucose and ketones for energy — or eating and fasting — could be beneficial.

So we're talking about some of the benefits of intermittent fasting and exercise is a good benefit too. You can add exercise while your fasting to help your body. Fasting and exercise is the optimal way to boost your health and body composition. Exercising before breakfast is optimal for your health because you're exercising during your fasting. You shouldn't get up and immediately have breakfast after a fast. To reap the most benefits you should fast between 16-18 hours and so that means you wouldn't normally eat when you first get up. So that's what makes exercising such a good benefit because you can exercise when you first get up. You don't want to eat directly after exercising either. If you wait a couple hours after exercising before you eat it helps you to burn fat quicker.

According to Dr. Mark Mattson at John Hopkins University, "If you don't expose yourself to mild bioenergetic stress, whether it's exercise or fasting intermittently, then it's not so good for your cells, particularly as you age. You aren't tapping all of the processes that help cells resist stress, function efficiently and fight disease." So exercise stresses the muscles making them more efficient. Intermittent fasting and exercise promotes a healthy immune system.

We've talked before about how God created your body to work and how each part of your body functions. Well God also created your immune system to help your body fight off germs and diseases. So intermittent fasting also helps your immune system and it's probably the number one benefit because you're always using your immune system.

The old and damaged cells in your immune system are recycled and replaced with new ones. Fasting helps your body to focus on this cleanup and it gets rid of toxins and excess calories.

Benefits on your immune system are:

Reduced aging of your immune system

Lower white blood cell numbers

Lowered inflammation

Protection against inflammatory related conditions

I hope you're beginning to see that every time we eat, our body has to use energy to metabolize food and convert food into fuel. Intermittent fasting boosts your immune system because it helps with the removal of waste in your body. The waste removal allows your body and organs to run more effectively, which leads to stronger immune function.

Fasting lowers white blood cell counts, and in turn gets the immune system to start producing new white blood cells. White blood cells are a key component of your body's immune system. Fasting is all about getting your body to switch over from glucose metabolism to ketone metabolism. Ketone metabolism seems to bring a host of health benefits. The trick is getting our bodies to switch over to it. If we eat constantly, then our bodies happily subsist on glucose and never make the switch. Ketone uses protein and molecules to influence health.

I hope you're beginning to see that fasting is good for your body and sometimes your body just needs a reset. We eat so much during the day and we put so much in our bodies that we don't realize how it's harming our bodies.

The foods we eat can put toxins in our body and when the digestion process starts it's hard to function. When we do intermittent fasting it gives our body a reset and our bad cells are replaced with new ones and our metabolism is now replenished.

I'm sure if you're like me and sometimes you just stay tired and run out of energy well you're body is the same way. If you keep putting more bad than good stuff into it then it's going to get wore down and it's going to need a reset to function properly. That's how intermittent fasting works to replenish your body back to working like it should. By only eating certain times during the day it's like giving your body a much needed restart.

Like I mentioned before it might not be for everyone but everyone can do it. It's as simple as not eating anything after your dinner meal and when you wake up the next day you will have fasted at least 10-12 hours. Always make sure you're staying hydrated during this fast because you don't want to get weak from not eating. For those starting it the first time I would start slow and only do it for 6-8 hours. While you're sleeping is the biggest part of the fasting.

CHAPTER 5

How To Stay Fit

I'm sure we've all seen the diets and the pills that say you can lose weight and be healthier. I've never had to be on a diet to lose weight but I did try some pills to gain weight when I was in my 30's. I was so tired of people telling me I needed to gain weight and I ate a lot but never gained much weight. Well the pills didn't really help me to gain much weight and it was only short term because after I stopped taking them the few pounds I gained left.

It's not about the diets to either lose or gain weight it's about changing the way you do things. You have to change your mindset. Just because food is there and available doesn't mean you need to eat. However you go about eating you need to think about creating a healthy lifestyle that you will continue for the rest of your life. You don't have to give up the foods you love because you can still have pizza and Mexican but you just know you have to eat it in a different way.

When you change the way you've been eating you might not want as much of that Mexican food. I've never needed to lose weight until the past few years as I've gotten older and now that I'm living a healthier lifestyle I know what foods are easier on my stomach and gut to digest. I've gotten to love fruits and salads and I still eat my chocolate ice cream and other foods I love but know my limits and I'm not overworking my body like before. Don't deny yourself the foods you love just make sure you're putting more good than bad food into your body.

All of us have busy lives whether you have a job or you're retired, our lives always seem to stay busy. There are a few things you can include in your daily routines to help stay fit. In previous chapters we talked about God and how He designed our bodies to work. So the best way to start your day is with meditation and reading God's Word. You might say oh I don't have time and yet you do because you can find short chapters to read. Psalms and Proverbs are good books to read any time. As you start incorporating this into your morning ritual you will see that you do have time. I have to admit though that I also struggled with it until it became part of my morning ritual. It's also part of my nightly ritual too because after a long day we need to calm down before retiring to sleep. There's no better way to start your day than listening to God speak to you through reading His Word and no better way to end your day. It's helpful to meditate by reading God's Word so you will be at peace and have more energy before starting your day. Another benefit is that you're less stressed and have improved immune function and will be able to sleep better.

Another thing that's good to start your day is by drinking lemon water. You can drink your lemon water while you read God's Word! I'm not talking about the artificial lemon in the bottle you can buy. You need good filtered or bottled water and real lemons. Make sure you don't use tap water because it's not good for you and has toxins in it. Lemons are good for you because they flush out toxins that might be in your body. They also give you more energy and fights off inflammation. Meditating and drinking your lemon water is a good way to start ever day. Lemons have so many benefits and when you squeeze fresh lemons into good water it makes it even better for your body.

Some of the benefits of drinking lemon water:

Flushes Out Toxins

Balances PH Levels

Assists In Weight Loss

Is An Immune Booster

Helps With Digestion

Squeeze half of a lemon into 12-16 ounces of good water and you're set for your day.

When you drink lemon water you're actually helping to clean your body. The lemon juice will stimulate the enzymes in your liver which will help to flush out the toxins in our body. So starting your day with lemon water will actually reset your body as you prepare for your day.

Now let's talk about getting a good nights sleep. We talked earlier about meditation and how it will help you sleep good if you meditate before you go to sleep. There are many other things you can do also to get a good nights rest. You might think that sleeping good doesn't have anything to do with getting your body fit and healthy; however, it does because if your body has the right nutrients and is stress free you will get a good night's sleep. There are some people that do have health issues that keep them from sleeping good but there are things you can do to improve your sleep.

The main thing is to drink enough water before you go to bed so you will stay hydrated during the night. You drink water during the day to keep alert and drink water at night to reduce fatigue and help you to sleep better.

Try to eat healthier foods and those that are rich in vitamins and proteins. You need vitamins B and C and calcium, magnesium, iron, and zinc. Too much sugar, caffeine, and processed foods will cause insomnia and disrupt your sleep so choose the foods you eat wisely. In order for you to get a good nights sleep choose foods rich in vitamins and proteins.

Another way to get your body fit is to eat more frozen and fresh vegetables rather than the canned ones. With this fast paced world we live in things that are easy and fast seem better but not always. Opening a can of vegetables seems easier and quicker to cook than fresh or frozen and it might be but let's see which one is better for your body.

Fresh and frozen vegetables are both nutritionally good for you. You can also freeze vegetables from your own garden and always have good food on hand. Canned vegetables on the other hand are cooked more than frozen and so destroy a lot of their nutrients. Canned vegetables or fruits also have added sugar and salt. Eating any fruit or vegetables is making a good choice toward your health but just make sure and check the label if you're buying cans because you don't need a lot of added sugar or salt. According to the Harvard T.H. Chan School of Public Health, "a person needs anywhere between five and thirteen servings of fruits and vegetables every day." How many servings you actually get will depend on the person though because we're all made different. One thing for sure though you do need plenty of fruits and vegetables to maintain good health.

A few years ago my doctor suggested that I start taking Vitamin D and I just thought it was because I was getting older. It turns out that our bodies need Vitamin D and even though we get it from the sun, sometimes we don't get enough of it so we need supplements.

Vitamin D provides a lot of health benefits. It helps your body absorb calcium and plays an important role in immune and muscle health. Another benefit is that it aids in healthy teeth and bones. You can get vitamin D from the sun, from food, and supplements. Only a few foods naturally have vitamin D and that includes fatty fish, beef liver, cheese, egg yolks, and mushrooms. There are foods that are fortified with vitamin D and these include cereal, milk, and orange juice and eating these can increase your intake of vitamin D.

We call vitamin D a vitamin but it's actually a pro hormone

in that it helps the body to produce and regulate it's use of hormones. Our hormones are not just responsible for our energy and moods, they also regulate our appetite and our sleeping and waking cycles.

Vitamin D can also support your lung function. Studies show that vitamin D can actually help you to breathe more easily by allowing you to take in more oxygen with each breath.

Another benefit is that it will help your teeth. You can end up with whiter and cleaner looking teeth and suffer from fewer problems. So whether you get vitamin D from the sun or food or supplements it has quite a few good benefits for your health.

Who loves coconut or doesn't love coconut? Whether you like it or not, there are quite a few health benefits with using coconut. I've never liked coconut in food but recently I found out how beneficial it is for your well being. Now I drink coconut milk in my coffee and sometimes use coconut oil.

Coconut oil has many benefits including that it will boost your immune system. Coconut oil has many uses from cooking to beauty and to skincare. You can add coconut oil to your food to reduce inflammation, hydrate your body and skin, boost your metabolism and give you more energy. You can add some coconut oil to your oatmeal and it makes for a good breakfast plus it can help in weight loss. I've had this with my oatmeal and believe me it gives you energy for the day.

You can also use coconut oil for skincare. It will calm sunburned skin and will also help with bug bites. It can also be used with your nightly moisturizer and you will see a reduction in age spots and wrinkles.

Coconut oil is also good for your teeth and gums. It has been used for years to promote dental health in a process called oil pulling where it gets rid of bacteria that may lead to tooth decay and bad breath. Oil pulling is a process where you swish it around in your mouth and around your teeth. It has a cleansing effective to reduce bacteria and plaque.

We've all grown up using fluoride in our toothpaste and hearing how it helps to prevent cavities. I bet you didn't know the toothpaste you've been using is toxic if it has fluoride in it. When I found out I quickly found a non fluoride toothpaste. It's so toxic that the FDA requires a warning on all toothpastes.

Dentist Tony Lees says, "in the scale of toxicity, fluorides fall between arsenic and lead" and he also said "dental fluorosis is not just a cosmetic problem, but the visible sign of chronic fluoride poisoning, and children are more vulnerable than adults." Fluoride is also in the water systems and was used to prevent cavities; however, in countries without fluoridated water they have less cavities. That's why I mentioned earlier to not drink the tap water and to get good water.

Another thing that's bad for our health is aluminum. I bet you didn't realize your putting aluminum in your body every time you use antiperspirant. They contain aluminum salts that plug your body pores and prevent you from sweating.

Chemist Randy Schueller says the aluminum compounds "not only reduce wetness by blocking your underarm swear ducts, but they also minimize body odor by inhibiting the bacteria that feed on your sweat and cause even more of it." I've also changed to a non aluminum antiperspirant. You need to be careful what you're putting in your body whether it's food or things you're putting on your body.

I'm sure in this day and age we've all heard of essential oils and probably used some of them. They can have a positive impact on your health and well being as long as you use them safely.

Essential oils are basically plant extracts. They're made by steaming or pressing plants together to trap the compounds responsible for their fragrance. Michelle Davila a naturopathic doctor says, "one way they work is through our sense of smell." Aromatherapy has been used for years and it's the process of using essential oils for therapeutic benefits. When inhaled the scent molecules in essential oils travel from the nerves to the brain and impact the emotional center of the brain.

Some of the most popular essential oils are:

Lavender-it helps to relieve stress and anxiety and promotes good night's sleep
Tea Tree-wound healing and used for acne and insect bites
Peppermint-relieves tension headaches
Lemon-mood booster

Essential oils also possess other benefits such as being an antibiotic, anti-inflammatory and antioxidants.

Many essential oils have antioxidants and they help prevent damage to cells. Essential Oils can lower stress and anxiety as well as relieve nausea and encourage sleep. Essential Oils are a helpful addition to your healthy lifestyle.

Exercise is another way to get fit and have a healthy lifestyle. Exercise and physical activity are a great way to feel better and boost your health. Have you ever been doing something like working in flower beds and then the next day your muscles are hurting? Well I always say you've used muscles you haven't used in awhile and that's true. If you are sitting a lot and not moving around then when you go to do something strenuous your muscles will feel the effect.

Believe me I'm right there with you because I sit most of the day at work and then when I'm doing something laborious my body feels it. On days when I'm always up and walking or doing work at my house my muscles don't hurt as much. Before I started walking after I got off work my legs would always ache and now with doing exercise it's much better.

Exercise not only keeps you in shape but it also keeps your body working better. If you regularly do some kind of exercise it will improve your muscle strength and endurance. I've also noticed that when I'm exercising I seem to have more energy to get things done. Exercise will give oxygen and nutrients to your body and will also help out your heart and lungs. I hope you're noticing that a lot of what we do in our life is so inter-related whether it's what we're eating or if we're exercising. It all affects our body in some way.

CHAPTER 6

Southern Belle Hacks

I'm from the South and have always lived in the south even though I have friends on the west coast and in the north and have visited them occasionally. What I found out is some of the food we eat in the south is similar but then there's some food that's different. People from the south have always been know as warm and inviting and always eager to bring some kind of casserole to a neighbor. We drink our sweet tea whereas some of my northern friends drink their unsweetened tea. Bless their hearts! Unsweet tea is the healthiest option though because it gives you antioxidants and is a good weight loss option. if you're going to coat your sweet tea with pounds of sugar, another option is to add honey instead of sugar because we know sugar isn't that good for you. Honey is also rich in antioxidants and has lots of nutrients and is better for your blood sugar levels.

Southern food has definitely transformed over the past few years and it has both healthy and unhealthy foods. The southern cuisine has its roots in plant based foods. Greens, sweet potatoes and vegetables haven't gone out of style and restaurants focus on vegetable based menus. Whatever you eat though it's all about balance! Everything is good for you in moderation and nothing in excess is good for you!

In the south you will find a lot of different kinds of tea that we drink. One kind I grew up with is Sun Tea. You basically let the sun make the tea for you. Take about 4 tea bags and 1 quart of water in a glass container and sit it out in the sun for about 2-4 hours and you will have the best tasting tea ever.

Tea is generally one of the healthiest choices no matter what kind you drink. It's almost calorie free and full of flavor. True teas come from a plant called camellia sinensis and the classification of the teas depends on how the tea leaves are processed. The most true teas are black, green, and white teas. There is also a variety of popular herbal teas made from flowers, leaves, and grains. Green tea is one of the oldest and healthiest drinks and one of my favorites. Green tea has antioxidants and can help brain function and may prevent heart disease. There's also mint tea and this is one of the most beneficial herbal teas. Mint teas can help with sore throat as well as your digestion and will help with weight loss because it stimulates your digestive enzymes and it absorbs nutrients and it's also a stimulant. Brigham and Womens Hospital says "some of the best herbal tea for gut health include peppermint, chamomile, anise, turmeric, fennel, coriander, and caraway."

Southern foods could be called comfort foods because it reminds us of warm and fuzzy things like Grandma's cooking and the simpler things in life.

Collard greens are an all time southern favorite. They're rich in beta carotene and full of antioxidants. They're not unhealthy on their own but many recipes call for adding fat and sodium in the form of ham hocks , bacon, and butter. So you can still make them healthy by just adding a little salt to boiled collard greens and adding red pepper flakes, and garlic for taste.

Another southern favorite is grits and if you're not from the south then you probably wonder what grits even are. Grits became important in the south because every farm grew corn. There are plenty of ways to make grits but their unique flavor is boiled with cream, butter, and salt for taste.

Another staple in the south is chicken pot pie. It's one of those meals that pleases everyone. It provides a level of comfort like none other with its pastry, broth, chicken, and vegetables all in one sitting.

We can't forget about peanuts and coke because in the south they just seem to go together. It's a sweet and salty snack that we all had in our childhood. Now we can't forget about boiled peanuts and this is a true southern experience. They can't be mushy or raw when cooked and it's best to eat them outside.

Another southern food is pecan pie and depending from where you're from the pronunciation is always different. It tastes so good though with butter, karo syrup, and pecans. You can also make it with honey and maple syrup so it will be a little healthier because we know added sugar isn't good for you.

We all have traditions for what we eat on New Years hoping to make the new year a great one. In the south you will find us eating black eyed peas, corn bread, collard greens, ham or pork hoping we will have good luck. Black eyed peas represent coins and luck, collards represent green for money, cornbread represents gold, and pork represents richness. They're also healthy for you and are full of nutrients.

Collard greens are part of the vegetable family and have cancer protective effects. Cornbread made with whole wheat flour and stone ground cornmeal contributes fiber and black eyed peas are also rich in fiber. They also contain plant substances which protect our cells from damage. It's all healthy but I'm sure most southerns will tell you they eat it for the tradition. I've eaten this as long as I can remember and never knew how many healthy nutrients it contained.

Cornbread in the south is also called hoe cakes and it has nothing to do with cakes! Hoe cakes are little cornmeal pancakes that are crispy around the edges. We serve them warm and top with butter and they can be eaten any time of the day. This classic southern recipe is basically fried cornbread. They were a staple of early American life in the South.

Another southern tradition is buttermilk.

I grew up eating cornbread mixed up in a glass of buttermilk. You always need pinto beans too with cornbread and buttermilk. You can also mix up cornbread and pinto beans on your plate and drink a glass of buttermilk or sweet tea.

Buttermilk does have health benefits. It's a good source of calcium and calcium supports the growth and maintenance of strong bones and teeth. By drinking buttermilk you can have improved blood pressure and improve bone and oral health. Vitamin A is in buttermilk and boosts your immune system and keeps your lungs, heart, and kidneys healthy. Buttermilk also has Vitamin B and this vitamin will give you more energy.

Benefits of drinking buttermilk:

Reduces Acidity
Fights Constipation
Cooling Effect
Prevents Dehydration
Helps in Detoxification
Provides Vitamins and Nutrients
Rich in Calcium
Reduces Blood Pressure
Reduces Cholesterol
Prevention of Diseases

As you can see drinking buttermilk can help you in many ways. So give buttermilk a try even if you're not from the south and see how it can help you. If you're needing more energy this is a good energy booster plus it will help your immune system. It's a good way to put a lot of calcium and nutrients in your body.

Something else the south is famous for is sweet potatoes and you will find us eating sweet potato anything and everything. There's your sweet potatoes and then theres sweet potato pies and casseroles and don't forget sweet potato fries! I've eaten them all and love them all. I've made many sweet potato casseroles over the years and mine is usually topped with melted marshmallows. There's nothing like sweet potato fries to go with a cheeseburger and you don't need ketchup because they're good just like they are.

Sweet potatoes in any form are also healthy for you and have plenty of health benefits! Antioxidants are a big health benefit you will find plus a lot of nutrients. When you get antioxidants from food rather than supplements they work better in your body. Of course anything in its natural form will work better.

Potassium is another benefit and sweet potatoes have the highest source of any vegetable. We need potassium because it helps our nerves and muscles as they communicate with each other. It offsets the damage that sodium has on our blood pressure. It also helps to protect and regulate your kidneys. It's also transports nutrients into our cells.

Sweet potatoes also have the highest count of beta carotene. Why is that important you ask! Because foods that have it will convert it to Vitamin A and our bodies need Vitamin A. Our bodies will only convert as much Vitamin A as it needs but we first need foods with beta carotene. Vitamin A is important for our vision, growth, cell division, reproduction, and immunity so it's important to eat foods that will give us Vitamin A.

Living in the south also means there will be plenty of casseroles around. We love to make and eat casseroles. They're all pretty simple to make and you just change out the vegetables. It can be a green bean casserole or a squash casserole and plenty more that I could name.

Squash casserole is probably close to my favorite and squash is good and healthy for you too. It's packed with plenty of nutrients. First thing about squash that comes to mind is that it's low calorie and it helps in weight loss. It's free of fat and cholesterol plus you will feel full longer when you eat squash. It's rich in vitamins A, B, and C. It's also rich in minerals like iron, magnesium and potassium plus it has antioxidants.

Another good southern casserole is the green bean casserole and green beans are good for your health. One of the main benefits of green beans is helping your heart. If your heart is healthy it will bring health to other organs. Green beans contain antioxidants that help prevent blood clots in arteries and veins. Another good benefit of green beans is that it help with those with diabetes. They assist in managing and regulating the symptoms of diabetes because they decrease sugar levels. Green beans have low calories and unsaturated fat so they help to lower cholesterol. Green beans are also high in iron and we need iron to combat anemia.

We've been talking about southern food and what true southerners will eat at the dinner table. Now let's talk about "Southern Belles" and how they act. They have a certain attitude, appearance and manners. They will fake a smile without appearing fake. Southern gals have warmth, grace, and hospitality in their daily dress, speech and behavior. Southern women are in a class of their own. They're as sweet as their sweet tea until you refuse to have seconds of their meal. Southerners will have grits for breakfast, lunch and dinner. There's always a good barbecue somewhere in the south and they love a good dinner party. Southern gals will always have grits and collard greens and make enough food for an army. Southerners will use a lot of spices in making their food. Herbs have been used for food and medicine in the past and today Southerners use them for good living to season food or provide fragrances. Herbs can also be grown from seeds and one of the popular ones from the south is lavender. It's used to perfume bath and cosmetic products.

Southern Belles use pet names such as sweetie, sugar, honey, and darlin and they're always smiling. Southern Belles are smart, confident, always poised.

Biscuits and gravy are the ultimate southern food and don't forget the side of molasses. I grew up eating biscuits for every meal of the day with either gravy or molasses. You might think that's not very healthy and you probably think molasses has a lot of sugar. We've talked about how processed sugar is bad for you but the sugar content in molasses is far less sweet and molasses actually have a few health benefits. It contains more vitamins and minerals than your everyday sugar.

One tablespoon of molasses has 41 milligrams of calcium or 3 percent of your daily value, according to the USDA.

Calcium is very important for our bodies and we need it for strong bones and teeth. It plays an important role in how your muscles function and helps us to have healthy blood pressure. Molasses is also loaded with magnesium and potassium. Magnesium will help with your blood sugar and blood pressure and potassium will keep your fluid levels balanced. They also have several B vitamins which helps our body convert food into energy.

Even though biscuits and gravy are a southern staple it's high in calories and saturated fats; however, you can make it healthier. When making your gravy use lower fat milk such as skim or unsweetened almond. Also use poultry seasoning and whole wheat or white wheat flour. When making your biscuits use wheat flour too. You can also add healthy side items to go with your biscuits such as boiled eggs or fruit. Molasses versus gravy with your biscuits is up to you whether you want to make your gravy healthier or eat molasses that already has health benefits.

There's nothing better in the south than a good ole barbecue. Believe it or not your pork barbecue does have some health benefits for your body.

Pulled pork that is used in barbecues are high in proteins. This is the main benefit if you want to lose weight or maintain your weight. It also has magnesium which is good for the growth of teeth and bones.

Pulled pork also promotes better metabolism which causes you to lose fats in your body. Metabolism usually happens while we sleep so you will lose those body fats while you're sleeping. Pork boosts your immune system because it contains zinc. We all know that our immune system keeps away diseases. It's also an energy booster due to all the proteins.

Pork has many vitamins and minerals that your body needs to function like iron and zinc. The high quality proteins in pork are amino acids and building blocks for creating new muscle. Barbecue pork contains many vitamins, minerals, and other substances such as protein and amino acids that are beneficial for you. They help to promote body building as well as producing red blood cells. So, as you see there are many health benefits in pulled pork for you! So go enjoy your next barbecue!

CHAPTER 7

Fruits and Vegetables

We've talked a lot about what's healthy for your body and talked about different foods. Now we're going to talk about my favorite fruits and vegetables! I probably love fruits and vegetables more than meat. I eat some kind of fruit every day.

Vegetables and fruit are an important part of a healthy diet and we need to eat a variety of them every day. No single fruit or vegetable contains all the nutrients our body needs so quantity doesn't matter.

There are probably about 9 different families of fruit and vegetables and each with different nutrients that are beneficial to our health. We need to eat a variety of types and colors to get the mix of nutrients our bodies need. Plus it will give you a colorful plate and an eye appealing meal. Keeping fruits and vegetables in your diet has many benefits. They can lower blood pressure, reduce heart disease and stroke, lower digestive problems as well as having a positive effect on blood sugar. Eating non-starchy vegetables and fruits may even help with weight loss because they help with blood sugar spikes which will increase hunger.

Eating fruits and vegetables can also keep your eyes healthy and may prevent cataracts and eye disease. If you're not already eating fruits and vegetables why not try it and see what a difference it will make. I wasn't that much of a fruit person until I saw the benefits and now I eat several different kinds of fruit and it's even giving me more energy and it compliments your meals.

Here are some tips to help you get started eating fruits and vegetables if you're not already eating them.

Keep fruit where you can see it
Explore the produce isle and choose something new
Skip the potatoes
Make it a meal

Variety and color are keys to a healthy diet and thus the start of a healthy lifestyle. On most days try to eat at least one serving from dark green leafy vegetables, yellow or orange fruits and vegetables, red fruits and vegetables and beans and citrus fruits.

Try cooking new recipes that include more vegetables. Salads, soups and stir fry are some good ideas. I've started eating salads for lunch and having some kind of fruit and now it's my daily routine.

Fruits and vegetables contain indigestible fiber which absorbs water and expands as it goes through your digestive system. It can calm symptoms of an irritable bowel and even help prevent diverticulitis according to the New England Journal of Medicine. People who ate more than 5 servings of fruit and vegetables had a 20% lower risk of coronary heart disease and stroke according to the Journal of Human Hypertension. As you can see adding fruit to your diet is a good healthy benefit. Eating fruit with your vegetables will give you more essential vitamins, minerals, antioxidants and fiber.

There are some fruits that give you more health benefits than others.

The ones on the top of the list that you need to be eating are:

Strawberries

Blueberries

Watermelons

Bananas

Raspberries

Avocados

Prunes

I've probably eaten all of these except for avocados and prunes. Watermelon is an all time favorite to eat in the south.

Strawberries are a healthy and sweet fruit and an excellent choice for diabetics.

"Strawberries are a great source of the antioxidant anthocyanin, which has been shown to reduce inflammation, oxidative stress, and insulin resistance which are all risk factors associated with type 2 diabetes," says Toby Smithson, Registered Dietician.

Blueberries are full of antioxidants and you can eat a handful at a time because they're as healthy as they are delicious. There's nothing better than a strawberry and blueberry pie!

Nothing better than a slice of watermelon at a summer picnic. It tastes good plus has healthy benefits. "Watermelon is high in lycopene, an antioxidant which studies suggest can lower the risk of certain cancers and improve heart health," says Rachel Rothman, MS, RD, CLEC. Lycopene helps give watermelon its red color and can be found in other foods like tomatoes, grapefruit, and papaya.

Bananas are the perfect fruit on the go because you can grab one and eat as you go on your way. Bananas will give you energy and are easy to digest.

Raspberries are the one fruit that's high in fiber. One cup of raspberries equals to eight grams of fiber. They're also full of antioxidants and Vitamin C. Raspberries are a fruit you should be eating every day.

No matter what your favorite fruit to eat is I've given you several healthy fruit options.

Vegetables are packed with a lot of nutrients, vitamins, fiber and minerals and by adding some to your diet it may help your overall health.

Tomatoes is technically considered a fruit but most people call them a vegetable. They contain a large amount of potassium and Vitamin C. Tomatoes also have compounds that aid in healthy eyesight.

I've always loved bell peppers and grew up eating them and never realized all the health benefits they have. They actually have more Vitamin C than oranges and they have B-6 and beta carotene. They have antioxidants that will help protect your eyesight.

Carrots are another healthy vegetable and I love eating carrots. Any soup that I make has to include carrots. I grew up hearing that carrots will help give you good eyesight and they have lots of good healthy benefits. They have 4 times the amount of daily recommended Vitamin A and they contain beta carotene.

Anyone who wants to stay fit and healthy knows that eating vegetables and fruits is essential to becoming fit and healthy. Eating lots of vegetables will give you lots of energy and will make you feel more active. They aid in body detox as they eliminate harmful toxins. Vegetables are rich in nutrients, fiber, antioxidants and a lot of natural minerals and vitamins. They are the key to cleansing your critical organs so let's start eating your veggies. I'm sure we all remember our parents telling us to eat our vegetables. If you don't have time to cook your vegetables there's organic vegetable juices to drink that are good in detoxification and cleansing.

There are some vegetables that are more healthier than others.

Spinach

Kale

Broccoli

Beets

Cabbage

Tomatoes

Asparagus

Sweet Potatoes

Brussels Sprouts

Bell Peppers

Some of these you might not like but if you can include a few of these with your other vegetables they will be very beneficial to your health. You will have higher energy levels, better skin health, reduced risk of disease, weight control and overall well being.

Broccoli is something I've eaten most of my life and didn't realize how healthy it really was. It's low in calories and rich in nutrients. Broccoli is loaded with Vitamin C, Vitamin K, fiber, and potassium and also has beta carotene, zinc, iron and magnesium. Broccoli has as much vitamin C as an orange and we know we all need the antioxidants we get from vitamin C.

Broccoli is high in fiber and helps your digestive system and can lower cholesterol. The potassium in broccoli is essential for the functioning of your nerves and heart contraction.

A study by Nutrition Research found that by consuming steamed broccoli regularly lowers the risk of cardiovascular disease by reducing the total amount of cholesterol in the body. So let's stay heart healthy by eating some broccoli.

Cabbage is another healthy vegetable that looks a lot like lettuce and you can use it in dishes like sauerkraut and coleslaw. It's packed with vitamins, minerals and antioxidants and is also low calorie. It contains powerful antioxidants that may reduce inflammation and it improves your digestive health. According to Healthline, Cabbage is rich in insoluble fiber which has been shown to increase the number of beneficial bacteria in the gut and these bacteria perform important functions like protecting the immune system and producing critical nutrients like vitamins K2 and B12. So eat more cabbage and have a healthy digestive system.

Red cabbage is an excellent source of potassium which is a mineral and electrolyte that your body needs to function properly. Potassium keeps blood pressure in a healthy range so increase your intake of cabbage to lower your high blood pressure. Cabbage is an exceptionally healthy food and it makes a tasty and inexpensive addition to your meals. Eating cabbage may help lower the risk of certain diseases and combat inflammation in your body.

Cabbage and lettuce may look similar but they're entirely different vegetables even though they're both healthy. Both are low in calories but cabbage is higher in nutrients except

Vitamin A and lettuce gives you the Vitamin A you need. So to get a variety of nutrients that your body needs eat cabbage and lettuce.

As we're talking about eating fruits and vegetables, let's not forget about dried fruit. With dried fruit you can always have it with you as a snack and it might not be as messy as the real fruit. Dried fruit tastes just as good as the real fruit if not better in my opinion. I've started taking it with me and when I need a snack before lunch I always have it with me.

Dehydrated fruit can be stored for much longer and it's also cheaper to purchase. The best dried fruits are apricots, cranberries, bananas, blueberries, and raisins. I've tried the bananas and blueberries and have even used the blueberries in my morning oatmeal. Whether you eat dried or fresh fruit getting s good amount of it in your diet will have a positive effective on your overall wellness. It will regulate your blood pressure, help your cholesterol and give you antioxidants and potassium and calcium. We still need to remember to watch our sugar content and we need to not overdo eating it. So make sure you watch your sugar intake with dried fruit because by eating too much you can make it become unhealthy for you. There are dried fruits without added sugar and they will generally have the same nutritional benefits as fresh fruit. Dried fruit has good health benefits as long as it doesn't have a large amount of added sugar. Remember we talked about how natural sugar on our foods is better for our bodies than the added processed sugars.

Tomatoes are a good source of the antioxidant lycopene which has many health benefits including reduced risk of heart disease and cancer. So the next time you're enjoying that good tomato on your hamburger remember it has a lot of health benefits plus it's protecting your heart. Tomatoes are an intensely nutritious plant food. They're an excellent source of Vitamin C and other antioxidants. Tomatoes are a rich source of lycopene, , lutein and beta carotene and these will protect the eyes. You might be surprised that tomatoes are low calorie and packed full of nutrients and have great benefits such as:

Great source of vitamins
Protect your heart
Support healthy vision
Boost digestive health
Help fend off diabetes complications
Contributes to skin health
Protects against cancer

As you can see by eating tomatoes it will give your body many nutrients. You might not think much about your skin like you do your other organs but did you know your skin is your biggest organ because it covers your whole body. Think about that for a moment. God created you in such a way that your skin is your biggest organ and covers your entire body. Tomatoes have lycopene which keeps your skin firm and gives its structure. According to Chicago Health, studies have shown that higher blood levels of lycopene are linked to lower death rates among people with metabolic syndrome (a cluster of risk factors that raise the chances of developing heart disease, diabetes, and stroke). So I hope you're seeing that lycopene in the tomatoes help a lot in your body.

Eating vegetables every day is important for your daily health. They provide essential vitamins, nutrients and minerals such as antioxidants and fiber. Certain vegetables may offer more health benefits to certain people depending on their diet, overall health and nutritional needs. According to Medical News Today, research shows that people who eat at least 6 servings of vegetables a day have the lowest risks of many diseases including cancer and heart disease.

Fermented vegetables also provide probiotics which is also good for your body. Probiotics are beneficial bacteria that are present in the body and in some foods and they may improve gut health. Some examples of fermented vegetables are cabbage, cucumbers, carrots, and cauliflower. We usually eat them in salads, sandwiches or a side dish. According to the National Center for Complementary and Integrative Health, probiotics may help with symptoms of irritable bowel syndrome.

Eating fruits and vegetables as part of your overall healthy diet are more likely to have a reduced risk of some chronic diseases. Adding vegetables to your diet can help increase your intake of fiber and potassium which are important nutrients that many people don't get enough of in their diet. Vegetables add bulk to your meal helping you to feel full and satisfied. So let's start eating plenty of vegetables that our body needs.

CHAPTER 8

Self Care

We've talked about how your body is created by God and how He created your body to work and what you need to do to keep your body fit. We've also talked about why you need to exercise and talked about a lot of food choices. So you have a basic outline on how to get your body in balance in order to be healthy. This can either be a short term goal or long term and it's all up to you! For me it has turned out to be a long term goal and it's a complete lifestyle change for the better. If you want a healthy lifestyle it first starts with being determined to take care of YOU!

Self care of YOU is centered around your spiritual, emotional, mental and physical well being. If one of these is out of sync then you need to take care of that before you can concentrate on the wellness of your body.

Self care is defined by Wikipedia as the process of taking care of oneself with behaviors that promote health and active management of illness when it occurs. Individuals engage in some form of self care daily with food choices, exercise, sleep and dental care.

We all need to take care of ourselves in all areas of our lives so that we will still be able to maintain our lifestyle and possibly make it even better. By taking care of ourself we can be healthy, we're able to do our job, we're able to help and care for others, and we can do all the things we want and need to accomplish.

Taking care of your spiritual needs is only a part of taking care of yourself but probably the most important. Practicing spiritual self care quiets the mind and calms the soul. If you've got stress from your day then it will relax and calm your body and soul. I try to read God's Word when I come home from working and to meditate and listen to God.

Physical care is taking care of your body, mental is taking care of your mind and spiritual is taking care of your soul. Caring for our soul is basically caring for our inner self and caring for ourselves on a deeper level. You need to tune in to your inner self to see what your soul needs to be healthy and happy.

Some ideas are:

Meditation
Commune with Nature
Practice Silence
Journal
Unplug from Technology

These will help you to get your inner soul in balance with the rest of your body. Remember when we started talking about your wellness we said it all starts with your soul.

It's always good to meditate whether it's doing yoga or studying God's Word and for me it's always reading my Bible. It clears my thoughts and relaxes me as I listen to God speak to me. Being somewhere quiet and in silence helps too.

Commune with nature whether you're walking around your neighborhood or you go to a park. Get out in nature and clear your head of any stressors. There's something about being outside and listening to the birds sing. Unplug from distractions around you and start a journal.

Another important aspect of self care is your emotional well being. It includes taking care of yourself and learning how to listen to your body when it's telling you to take a break from people or situations. Do you ever feel overwhelmed or frazzled and do you seem to be running yourself ragged? Well maybe you need to take some time out for just YOU! We stay so busy taking care of others that I think we sometimes forget to take care of ourselves. Emotional well being means you can identify and you're aware of what you're feeling. We can try to ignore or suppress our emotions but they will eventually come out in one way or another. If you find that you have emotional triggers in your life, you may need to say no to things and people that bring negativity in your life. We've all had stress and anxiety in our life but too much stress isn't good for your emotional well being. Try and find more healthy ways to process your emotions such as gratitude.

Find someone or something your grateful for each day. We talked about journaling before and it's a good healthy way to process your emotions. Finding healthy ways to process your emotions is key to your emotional self care. Focus on You and concentrate on what your needs are and take care of them either by taking a nature walk or venting to a friend or writing it down in a journal.

Self care is doing things that helps you live well and that will improve your physical and mental health. We all have the stressors from every day living and taking care of our emotional well being includes
managing stress, lowering your risk of illness and increasing your energy. Mental health affects how we think, feel, act, make choices, and relate to others. Understanding what caused or triggers your symptoms and finding what coping techniques work can help manage your mental health.

Some tips to help keep your emotional well being healthy include:

Get regular exercise
Eat healthy and stay hydrated
Make sleep a priority
Relaxing activities
Set goals
Focus on positivity

Did you know that 30 minutes of walking every day can boost your mood and improve your health? There have been a few times I have had a stressful work day and I will come home and immediately walk around the block just to clear my head. Remind yourself of things you're grateful for and thank God every day for His blessings on your life. Identify the negative and unhealthy thoughts and only concentrate on positive thoughts. Learn to say no and think on things you've accomplished during your day not on things you left undone. It's all about how you're thinking and how much negativity you allow in your life. Always try to focus on the positive.

We've talked about your spiritual, emotional, and mental well being and now let's talk about taking care of your physical prosperity. We need to take care of our physical needs because it will improve your physical condition and quality of life and will also prevent physical and mental illness. By keeping our physical well being in shape it will help our oneself and also help our relationships with others. Self esteem is how you value and respect yourself as a person. It affects how you take care of yourself emotionally, spiritually and physically.

Dorothea Orem, an American nurse defined self care as "the set of intentional actions that a person makes to control internal or external factors, which can compromise their life and later development." It's all about being aware and analyzing ourself. We need to Love ourself. You can't love others unless we love ourself first. In John 15:12 God commanded us to "love one another as I have loved you."

Physical self care is about taking care of our body because it's a vital part involved in our integral health.

We can do that in the following ways:

Sleep well and rest
Nourish yourself
Hydrate
Personal hygiene
Physical activity

Each person is unique and has their own special needs. There are many options of self care that will help you get to the well being of your body.

Self care should be made a priority; however, with most people including myself it's not a priority. People might think it's too expensive or might take too much of their time. Gracy Obuchowicz self care coach says, "most people approach self care from the thought "I'm going to make myself better," and that doesn't work." The simple fact is that we all need to be concerned about doing self care because it affects all areas of our body as well as how we live our lives and relate to others. Including healthy self care practices into your life can have lasting benefits. Some people might think self care and self improvement is the same thing but it's different. Self improvement is trying to fix something for the short term into the future but self care is an enjoyable experience right now and into the long term. Self care involves a healthy diet, exercise, sleep and a good work-life balance. Being with family and friends in a nurturing relationship is key to your health. Being involved in causes or organizations you care about can give your life meaning. So even though making time for self care is essential to performing well in all areas of our lives sometimes it's hard when you lead a super busy life. Nurturing our brains, bodies and spirits can help us be more effective in whatever we do.

We need to do self care on our terms not letting others tell us how to do it. Only you know what your body, spirit and soul need to survive.

You need to change the way you think about self care before you will be able to integrate it into your life. By changing your way of thinking you can bring small changes into your life and have greater peace, energy and joy. It's important to take time out of your day to check in on yourself. Once you determine which self care habits are best for you, practice them regularly for a balanced and healthy life. Hydration is important for your body and mind. Proper hydration plays a key role in regulating your body temperature, improving brain function and keeping your digestive system working properly. You can try using fruits you love in your water to encourage more water drinking throughout the day.

Going for a walk is a good thing to do especially for brain fog. Get outside and just enjoy nature. Taking a long walk can boost your mood, sharpen your thinking and help you to feel calmer. I love the outside and going for a walk after a stressful day always helps me.

What is a creative passion you've been wanting to do? That can be an amazing form of self care. You can paint, write, knit or take photos. You can also get an adult coloring book that's become so popular. Your environment has a direct impact on you whether you realize it or not. Having an organized uncluttered space can clear fatigue and help your mood.

Reading or doing a journal is a great way to practice self care and you can easily include this habit into your daily routine. Reading improves your memory, reduces stress and expands your vocabulary. Meditation is a good form of self care because you can sit in silence and look inward and give your mind a break from the busyness of life. This form of self care can lower your blood pressure, reduce stress, and improve your quality of life.

Sleep is a key component to a healthy mind so take a nap. Not getting enough of sleep can affect your health. Naps are a great way to recharge your body.

Writing down things you're grateful for can help you focus on the positive in your life instead of the negative. Thank God for the blessings in your life. "I give thanks to the Lord for he is good; for his steadfast love endures forever." I Chronicles 16:34. Practicing gratitude on a daily basis is the ultimate act of self care. Mindset is everything! It's important to reflect on the blessings in your life and express gratitude towards them. Regular exercise and moving your body can strengthen your mental health and boost self care. Physical health has a direct impact on mental health and can improve your mood, sharpen your mind and help you to live a happier lifestyle.

Now we're going to talk about things that we might do that will affect our mental health and prevent us from doing self care. It can be something as simple as being on social media too long or other little things and it will sabotage your mood and positivity. If you have a lack of physical activity and not exercising it could lead to depression. So let's keep walking to banish depression and mood swings. Toxic relationships are something else that will hurt our moods and well being. We need to always be in a positive environment and around uplifting people. If you never have time for You then you need to schedule at least 15 minutes of ME time. Everyone needs a mental break and just have time for themselves. Being a procrastinator can give you feelings of fear and anxiety and can cause stress and lower your mental well being. I'm a big procrastinator and I'm working on that.

One big thing that will prevent us from doing self care is your phone. We live in a society where our phones are our everything and we use them all of the time. We have forgotten how to do face to face conversation and look at our phones the whole time through dinner. If there's a lack of time that's preventing you from doing self care, then try setting boundaries on things that are interfering and if it's your phone then put it down.

Feeling guilty is another reason people don't want to do self care. We feel guilty for taking time for ourselves when there's so much that we need to do in our busy lives. You were born worthy of experiencing all that life has to offer so don't feel guilty for taking time to enjoy life. You deserve to have time to refresh and recharge. Another reason is lack of energy and believe me I've been there. After a busy work day and then taking care of your family and being tired and exhausted it's hard to think about doing anything else. You have to start doing little things at first and then your energy levels will increase and then that's when you add more. You will get more energy and you will feel like a new person. When you take time out for you then you will see who you really are and you will see what you love to do. The more you take care of yourself the better your self compassion will be toward others. Doing self care for ourselves will also boost our immune systems and I hope by now you understand how important your immune system is and why we need to be taking care of ourselves. By practicing self care you will have more to give others.

CHAPTER 9

Positive Thoughts

You have gotten this far in changing your mindset and changing your lifestyle so be proud of yourself and don't let anyone pull you down. You're strong and determined and you can do this! You don't have to give up the food you love or stop doing things you love. You just have to do things a different way with a different mindset. Keep telling yourself you can do it and don't listen to negative people. You're on your own track and you can invite others to go with you on this new journey.

You can even change some of your favorite foods to make them healthier. As long as you're putting more good nutrients in your body than bad you will be able to stay fit. Too much bad stuff as we've talked about can be bad for your body. Think about what you're eating and how you're eating. It will make all the difference in keeping your body in balance. Remember that's it's not just your body it's also your spirit and soul. Everything needs to be in balance and fit to maintain your new healthy lifestyle. You need to put on a new way of thinking as well as keeping your emotional well being in shape along with being aware of the foods you're putting in your body. Keep everything in balance to become a better and new YOU!

Your whole body will thank you for wanting to get fit and get everything in balance. By becoming fit your body will be free of chronic diseases. Becoming fit physically can also help you to become fit emotionally. If you're eating the right food and keeping your body in balance, you will be able to keep your body strong and you will be able to cope with stress and illness.

Eating good and exercising will help you to stay in good health and have a good immune system which will help you to be able to fight off disease and illnesses.

Being healthy and keeping your body in balance should be a part of your lifestyle. Feeling good about yourself will help your self esteem and your image. It's not just about being physically fit it's also about being emotionally and mentally fit. Like we've been talking about it's about getting everything in balance.......your spirit, soul and body are all connected. So changing to a healthy lifestyle will affect every aspect of your body. You will need a powerful attitude to change to getting your body where it needs to be. Staying positive and being positive can boost your energy, give you inner strength and also inspire others around you.

Becoming healthy and staying fit can help you as you grow older. It can make you feel more confident now that you're taking care of your body and keeping everything in balance. Exercise can even keep you in a great mood because when you exercise you're releasing hormones to your brain that enhances your mood. Eating foods that are good for you and staying physically active may help you to reach and maintain a healthy weight and improve how you feel.

Improving your health also gives you some benefits.

More energy
Feel better about yourself
Manage stress better
Tone your body without losing your curves
Set an example for friends and family

You can set specific goals for yourself and move at your own pace. Getting fit and healthy isn't just about losing weight it's about getting your body in balance so it will be able to work more efficiently.

When your body isn't fit you can tell because you can tell something is off. We know our bodies and we can tell when something isn't right. You may stay tired or your digestive system may be off and you might mentally feel drained and can't concentrate. Becoming healthier and maintaining a healthy lifestyle will help you to feel better. The good news is that you don't have to completely change overnight. It may be a few simple changes will lead you in the right direction of improved well being.

Making changes to improve your health can have benefits for your body and mind. Your journey toward a healthier lifestyle involves making small changes that you believe are attainable for you to achieve.

Set small goals for yourself such as those below and then reach for higher goals.

Eat more vegetables
Swap in whole grains
Be more active
Control stress

You decide what's good for you and what you're capable of achieving and do things that make you happy because we know unhappiness affects your health.

There's not anything you need to give up and you just balance the good with the bad and make sure you have more good than bad. You can also have one free day where you can eat whatever you want. Saturday was always my free day where I would either eat pizza or Mexican. You can also have a rest day from exercise too because you don't want to get burnt out.

Your version of a healthy lifestyle is whatever you define it to be. Think about what makes you feel good and what brings you the most happiness. Start with small changes and then blossom into larger ones and that's how you will see success. A healthy lifestyle will help you feel better, can reduce the risk of some diseases and even lengthen your lifespan.

Having a healthy lifestyle means different things to different people and it's not a quick fix you may only do for a short amount of time. When you embark on getting healthy it should be for your entire life if you intend to stay healthy. For some people the wellness lifestyle means exercising more while to others it might be improving their sleep habits or nutrition. Healthy choices are part of your life long journey and isn't a quick fix.

When you're exercising regularly and sleeping better and making informed eating choices, your body and brain will function at their greatest capacity. By making smart decisions, you can make the most out of your day and reap the benefits of living a healthy lifestyle.

One of the primary benefits is weight loss or weight management. With even moderate weight loss you can improve your blood pressure and cholesterol levels. My goal to getting healthier wasn't weight loss even though I needed to lose a few pounds and overall I did lose weight and I'm still continuing to stay fit and maintain my healthy lifestyle. I've got more energy than before and my body feels completely better. I'm able to do things without being tired all the time. Sometimes we need a change in our lives to help us to get to where we need to be.

Sleep is a part of us being fit and I would guess a lot of us don't get a good nights rest. I probably don't always get a good nights sleep. A good nights sleep will determine your energy level for the next day. So if you don't get a good nights sleep a lot of times you will have low energy. It's recommended that we get at least 7 hours of sleep and I'm sure a lot of us don't get 7 hours of sleep a night.

Regular physical activity results in longer, better quality sleep according to the National Sleep Foundation. Sleep is part of your healthy lifestyle and can be improved through exercise and eating right. Regular physical activity will result in longer and better quality sleep. Those who exercise regularly also lower their risk of developing sleep disorders.

Your sleep quality and energy levels can be improved with a wholesome diet. Limiting your caffeine can also improve your sleep. The more sleep you get the more your energy levels will rise.

Staying fit will also benefit your mental health. Exercise and healthy eating can help you manage stress which will also improve your mood. Not getting enough sleep will also affect your mood so that's another reason why we all need to get a good nights sleep. Aerobic exercise also boosts your heart health and we know how important it is to have a healthy heart. The longer you have a healthy lifestyle and stay fit the less likely you are to develop diseases.

We all know that when you change anything in your life it's going to be tough in the beginning and it will require a lot of determination and motivation. What sounds more fun your friends eating out and partying or you walking around the block or being on the treadmill? You've got to set your mind to it and disregard what your friends might be doing because you don't want to get distracted from your goal. You have determined to get fit and start on a healthy lifestyle so don't back down because your body is counting on you to stay strong. It's going to be tough but you can do it.

We're all human and sometimes we make less than healthy choices. If we can eat smart, exercise, and manage stress, you'll feel better and be ready for an active and healthy future. Having a healthy lifestyle will give you a better quality of life. By making daily small changes at the beginning you will start to see how it affects you because you may have extra confidence and just be happier.

Being healthy from the inside will move outwards and it will influence your emotional side. Feeling great about yourself from the inside to the outside is the key to living a more abundant, happy and confident life.

Times are tough in our economy and if you're trying to start living a healthy lifestyle it will be really tough. Any change you embark upon will be work and getting healthy is no different. We live in an unhealthy world because people seem to be eating whatever they want and either don't care or don't think how what they eat affects their body. The fast food places make it so easy and they're not that healthy and you can drive through and pick up your dinner. I used to do it all of the time until I woke up and realized what I was doing to my body and then decided to start eating differently and to get my body fit and in shape. I know how hard it is to have a healthy lifestyle with correct eating habits and exercise while your friends are indulging in all the foods you used to eat. You don't have to stop eating foods you love even though I did stop eating some foods in the beginning. As long as you're putting more good foods in your body than bad you will be on the right track to getting fit. After you get your body fit and everything in balance then you will just need to maintain it and continue on a healthy lifestyle. Staying healthy isn't just for your body because it will affect your emotional and mental well being also. Set some goals for yourself and stick to them!

Having a healthy lifestyle isn't just about eating nutritious foods. It's also about being physically active and getting enough sleep and focusing on your mental health. We talked about setting goals for yourself before so make them specific, attainable, measurable and realistic. Unless they're specific you might not even start on a healthy lifestyle because the goals you chose were too hard and out of reach.

Getting healthy and maintaining your health is worth the work it involves and comes with several great benefits such as:

Improve your physical health
Improve your mental health
Get more energy naturally
Boost your mood
Prevent disease and health issues
Always have goals to work toward

Eating the right foods in combination with physical activity and adequate sleep is a recipe for a healthy body.

Achieving a healthy lifestyle involves not only eating the right foods but also how much physical activity you engage in as well as engaging in self care. Try to achieve one thing at a time by setting some kind of goals. Reaching your goals can help you feel accomplishment and boost your self confidence.

A healthy lifestyle involves choice and action which means the choices you make and the actions you take can lead to a healthier lifestyle. Making positive choices in the areas of physical fitness, stress and and nutrition and acting on them will promote a sense of self worth, happiness and overall well being.

We've all heard the phrase "living your best life" but what exactly does that mean? That means different things to different people and each person's "best life" is determined by what they see as what will make them happy and content. It might be to get a new vehicle, make more money or lose weight. All of us want to be the best version of ourself that we can be.

When you decide to dedicate yourself to living your life to the fullest, you can overcome anything. Each day is an opportunity for greatness and we need to make the most of every day. Be thankful for every day your given because tomorrow isn't promised. Proverbs 27:1 "Boast not thyself of tomorrow; for thou knowest not what a day may bring forth."

Being positive can change a person's entire outlook on life. When you're living life to the fullest that's when you are the most in tune with yourself. Getting healthy and keeping your whole body in balance starting with your soul and spirit is one way you can really get in tune with yourself. When you get everything fit and in balance from the inside and out you're living more of a life of bliss and contentment. Be determined and stay positive and you can do it and you will be able to maintain a healthy and fit lifestyle.

CHAPTER 10

Tips and Tricks

We talked about how lemons and lemon water is good for you so be sure to include some lemon water with your meals and drink water throughout the day.

Exercise before you eat your breakfast. I will normally do some sit-ups and push-ups. I would start with 5 and then increase up to 20 as you can.

The breakfast I chose for my new healthy lifestyle is below.

Bowl of Oatmeal
Fresh Fruit
Tablespoon of Coconut Oil
1 piece of toast with jam
Coffee
Juice

I use Quaker Oats and I add almond coconut milk in my oats before cooking them in the microwave.

I put a teaspoon of coconut oil in my oats and add any kind of fresh fruit chopped up or sliced. You can use fresh fruit or frozen fresh fruit because it's both good.

I use Ezekiel 4:9 bread for my toast. It's flourless whole grain.

You can also add a cup of Greek low fat yogurt with your breakfast.

Some people might skip breakfast and just eat lunch. If you're doing intermittent fasting you might be skipping both meals and just be eating dinner. I usually didn't eat much for lunch and my big meal would always be dinner with the family.

Here are some lunch menu ideas.

Salad
Fresh fruit
Lemon water

Turkey sandwich
Bowl of fruit
Lemon water

I usually get the ready made salad bowls and they have lettuce and anything from eggs, bacon bits, ham, turkey, dressing in them. You can always make your own. Be creative!

The Turkey sandwich I would make with the Ezekiel 4:9 bread with a slice of cheese, lettuce, tomato and mayonnaise.

As you see I'm including fruit with just about anything I'm eating for breakfast or lunch. Since dinner is the family meal I would eat my normal and maybe change it up in different ways. Using less salt and low fat options will always work.

I'm sure you're thinking like I did about what you're supposed to do if you get hungry. Well you can snack in between meals and once your body gets used to your new routine you won't get as hungry. Make sure whatever you're eating as a snack that you watch the added and processed sugars. My go to snack food is either yogurt or dried fruit.

We had mentioned Oil Pulling before but didn't go into much detail. Oil pulling is swishing oil around in your mouth to remove bacteria and promote oral hygiene. Oil pulling will clean and whiten your teeth. I use coconut oil about a tablespoon and usually swish it around for about 5 minutes. When you finish your swishing remember to spit it out in a paper towel and throw it away because if it goes down the sink it will clog it up.

The main benefit is that it reduces the amount of harmful bacteria in your mouth. The bacteria in your mouth can cause plaque. Having some plaque is ok but if it gets out of hand it can cause other problems.

The way oil pulling works is simple. When you're swishing the coconut oil around any bacteria will get caught up and dissolved in the oil. To get the benefits you need to keep the oil moving around in your mouth anywhere from 5-20 minutes. That gives the oil time to work and to pull out the toxins. You should always brush your teeth after oil pulling and not before.

There's no right or wrong way to oil pull but just make sure you're moving the oil around in your mouth. As you're swishing it around in your mouth you need to force it through your teeth. You want to make sure it gets all the toxins in your mouth.

Now that we're talking about keeping your teeth free of toxins, let's talk about the toothpaste you use. If you're using a toothpaste that has fluoride in it you need to get one that is fluoride free. I know growing up we all had our parents and dentists that told us how fluoride would prevent cavities and it might have been creating them.

There are lots of different toothpastes that are fluoride free and the one I use is xylitol and it's really good.

Xylitol is a sugar alcohol found in plants and trees. Xylitol can have good dental benefits.

Fluoride is a toxic chemical and it's considered a hazardous waste by the EPA. It's so toxic that there has to be a warning on toothpaste telling users not to swallow it and if they do to call poison control. It's the same ingredient as in rat poison.

Fluoride is also in our tap water and that's why I only drink bottled water. Hiltler even fluoridated the drinking water in concentration camps to sedate the prisoners.

Excess exposure to fluoride has been shown to cause many health issues such as bone and joint issues.

Fluoride free toothpastes clean your teeth and remove any buildup. It targets the bacteria in your mouth with ingredients like calcium phosphates.

Preserving your teeth and reducing cavities is based on your dental hygiene and the toothpaste you use.

Now let's talk a bit about mouthwash. We all use some kind of mouthwash to keep our breath fresh. I wonder how many use hydrogen peroxide to rinse out your mouth. I use the food grade because it might be a little safer. Either one will whiten your teeth as well as kill any bacteria in your mouth. Always make sure you don't swallow it.

It has many uses from soothing a sore throat, reducing

gum inflammation to whitening teeth. It has antibacterial properties in it that can help your body fight off many things. It's also a powerful disinfectant to help canker sores in your mouth from getting infected.

Hydrogen peroxide can reduce gum inflammation when used with regular brushing and flossing. To get the most health benefits make sure you swish it around the front of your mouth when you're gargling so it reaches your front teeth and gums.

Always make sure you're diluting it with 2 parts water. You want to swish it around your mouth for at least 60 seconds to get the maximum benefit. Hydrogen peroxide is something everyone already has so it's very versatile when you can also use it as a mouthwash. It has a cleansing benefit when used in your mouth as long as it's diluted first.

We had briefly mentioned about aluminum being in our antiperspirants. Aluminum will enter our body through our sweat glands. Antiperspirants use aluminum so we will sweat less.

Aluminum in small amounts will not harm you; however, large amounts will cause health issues.

The aluminum free deodorant I use is called native and its all natural and I love it. It works really good.

We don't need aluminum to be getting in our bodies through our sweat glands and we can also keep our guts clean and our sweat won't smell.

Aluminum isn't good for us and too much aluminum in our bodies can cause toxicity. So why would you want to use deodorant or antiperspirant that has aluminum in it.

When you have aluminum in your antiperspirant it will block your sweat glands and you won't be sweating.

Why would you want to block your sweat glands because that's just part of how your body works to remove toxins.

I'm sure some people don't like to sweat and make think it's good to block your sweat glands but you need to look at the long term benefit or side effect. Having too much aluminum in your body can cause health issues for some people such as weakened bones and even memory loss leading to Alzheimer's.

We need to not only be careful what foods we put in our body but also be careful what we put on our body.

We had talked about lemons and lemon water and you can put any kind of fruit in your water if you don't like lemons.

I've had a really good lemon water recipe and you can find it in Michelle Moore Winder's book, Rock Your Red Carpet that you can find on Amazon.

I've had strawberry water and it's good too and probably my favorite next to lemon water. All you need is some fresh strawberries cut up and throw them in a bottle of fresh good water (not tap) and you will have a yummy drink.

Adding any kind of fruit to your water is refreshing plus you get antioxidants, vitamins and minerals and you're staying hydrated. You can also add vegetables and herbs to your water. Be creative!

Drinking water is always good for you and adding fruit to it has added benefits. It can help boost your immune system, increases energy, aids with digestion and promotes weight loss.

Drinking water to lose weight and improve your overall health is a good habit and one to add to your daily routine. They're so many choices on how to mix different fruits in your water.

Some of the benefits to drinking water include:

Natural appetite suppressant
Helps remove waste from the body
Replaces high calorie liquid intake

Drinking enough water keeps our body functioning properly and by staying hydrated we can flush out toxins and detoxify the body.

We've talked briefly about exercise and how we need to be moving around and exercising as well as eating correctly.

Exercise is our miracle cure that sometimes we neglect. I know it's a lot easier to just sit on the couch and watch tv than to be doing some form of exercise.

Scientific evidence even says that being physically active can help you to lead a healthier and happy life.

Exercise can boost your self esteem, mood, sleep quality and energy. You can't be in a bad mood after exercising because it will give you energy and it will pump you up. We need to make exercise part of our daily life and part of our routines.

For any physical activity to benefit your health, you need to be moving enough to raise your heart rate and breathe faster. People are less active nowadays because of our leisurely economy and technology has made our life easier. Inactivity or being sedentary is bad for your health.

The amount of exercise needed for health benefits depends on the goal, the type of exercise and the age of the person. Even doing a small amount is healthier than doing none. People who do at least 30 minutes of moderate exercise may also see a difference in their sleep and may actually sleep better. Pick an exercise you like and you will stick with it longer.

There are all different kinds of exercise that you can do to improve your well being and to keep you healthy. A lot of times I will take a stroll around the block and it will get my energy level up and my heart pumping because I might walk twice around the block.

You can be you and be creative and do exercises that are for you and ones that you enjoy. They can be outside or inside.

Here are a few examples:

Squats

Step ups

Lunges

Diagonal shoulder press

Forward press with ball

Whatever exercise or exercises you choose to do start out slow in the beginning and work up to more.

We need to be doing some kind of exercise daily because sitting all of the time isn't that good for you. I know because I sit all day at work and it's so easy to come home and sit watching tv or reading a book or being on your phone or computer.

When we sit too much it slows down our metabolism which affects the body's ability to regulate it's blood sugar, blood pressure and break down fat and may cause weaker muscles and bones.

Choose an exercise that will work for you and you can choose more than one and be motivated and faithful to do your exercises. I walk around the block in good weather and in bad weather I do sit ups or push ups. Exercising and eating correctly are essential to maintain your healthy lifestyle.

By now you have all the knowledge and the how to with having a healthy lifestyle.

I've showed you how God created your body to work and how it operates. You learned how your skin is your biggest organ and your brain is your operating system. Hopefully you've seen how your body is interwoven and operates with other parts of your body.

I've showed you how everything starts with your spirit and soul and then goes to your mind and body. It starts from the inside (your spirit) and goes to the outside (your body). It's all a process!

You have all the techniques to eat the correct food for your body. You learned how good water is for your body and how you can mix fruits with it for a delicious drink every day.

Remember to get rid of the Added and Processed Sugars in the food you eat! Make sure your gut is clean and do intermittent fasting to renew your body.

Exercise and eating correctly is the key to staying fit and healthy.

I wrote this book because I wanted to help others learn how to live healthy and stay healthy. I changed my whole way of how I was eating and changed my thinking in the process. Change your mindset and change the way you eat and watch not only what you eat but what you put on and in your body. Become a NEW YOU and live a life of BLISS and happiness!!

About The Author

Debbie Adams grew up on a farm in middle TN. Her greatest childhood memories were of sharing endless adventures with her father.... At the public library. The many trips she took all over the world with her Father kept her interest in reading alive. These trips took place in the dusty caverns of the public library. Her love of books inevitably led her to write. Her interest in health and personal experience led her to write this book.

It is the author's hope that this book will be a blessing on her readers' journey to better health and joy.

Made in the USA
Columbia, SC
26 August 2022